Kilimanjaro and

"If you're the kind of person who can usually find any excuse to talk yourself out of a great idea this book is the inspiration you need to get out of your comfort zone and make things happen."
— Helen Osler, author, Cameras of Kilimanjaro, Australia

". . . the writing is warm, familiar and humorous. *Kilimanjaro and Beyond* will challenge all who read it to consider how they too can make a difference, not only for others, but for themselves as well."
— Reader Views, Austin, Texas

"I loved this meticulous chronicle of one man's ascent (together with his son and another individual fulfilling a lifelong aspiration), to the highest mountain in Africa—at once so inspirational and courageous, so human and humane, and so deeply personal that the reader feels they are climbing right along with this small and highly determined group."
— Reverend Dr. Linda De Coff, author, Bridge of the Gods

"*Kilimanjaro and Beyond* is a beautifully written tale about a spiritual journey, a physical embarking, and so much more."
– GoodbooksToday.com

"Reading this book could change your life and set you off on a satisfying path of achieving your dreams and ambitions."
— Jeannie Walker, award-winning author, Fighting the Devil

". . . honest, funny, very engaging and truly written from the heart."
— Alysha Atma, Executive Director, Atma Foundation, Oregon, USA

"I am a local Kilimanjaro guide and I have always recommended your book to prospective clients and I have noticed they get to know a lot about the climb before embarking on it. It makes it an easier climb and works well for everyone."
— Robert, Kilimanjaro Guide, Tanzania, Africa

I Guess We Missed the Boat

A Travel Memoir

Barry Finlay

I Guess We Missed the Boat
Barry Finlay

Published by
Keep on Climbing Publishing

www.keeponclimbing.com

ISBN 978-0-9938910-2-1 (pbk)
978-0-9938910-4-5 (mobi)
978-0-9938910-3-8 (epub)

Copyright © Barry Finlay 2013

Illustrations and cover "photo": Rodel Castillo,
with exception of "Sexy Giraffe" by Magdalene Carson.

Design: Magdalene Carson.

No part of this book may be reproduced, stored in a retrieval system,
or transmitted in any form or by any means without
the prior written permission of the publisher or,
in case of photocopying or other reprographic copying, a licence from
Access Copyright (Canadian Copyright Licensing Agency),
One Yonge Street, Suite 800, Toronto, Ontario, M5E 1E5.

Cataloguing data available at Library and Archives Canada

Acknowledgements

I Guess We Missed the Boat is a mostly true travel memoir. Some events have been enhanced a little and the names of my in-laws and the friends included in the book have been changed. Their characteristics have also been exaggerated for the sake of the story. I want to thank them for all the laughs during our travels and for being kind enough to allow me to relate the stories. Of course, nothing can be accomplished without good friends, and I am very grateful for the contribution mine have made to the completion of this book. Many people have provided support and encouragement for my writing. Harvey Davey provided early comments on the manuscript, which resulted in a slight change in direction and a better book. Kip Kirby, whose writing skills I admire greatly, convinced me that the stories might be funny to other people besides me. Stacey Black offered enthusiastic and supportive feedback on the manuscript. Thank you to the GSPH team that was initially instrumental in getting this book off the ground. Special thanks to John Stevens, the personable editing guru, who provided suggestions and editorial comments to ensure my stories made sense and that the grammar and spelling were readable, and to Magdalene Carson at New Leaf Publication Design, who created the cover, giraffe illustration, and page design and formatted the book for publication. Rodel Castillo did a masterful job on the illustrations, which, I think, help bring some of the stories to life and make the characters more real. Robin Chu was my official photographer and provided the portrait. I would be remiss if I didn't thank our travel agent, Ann Black at Award Travel, who has sent us off on our adventures in an always professional way. I was also encouraged to write another book by the success of *Kilimanjaro and Beyond: A Life-Changing Journey*. Thank you to those who bought my first book and for the extremely positive feedback, and for the contribution your purchase has made to our project to help some young women and youth in Africa start small businesses. Finally, thank you to my wife and travelling companion of over forty years, Evelyn, who patiently read draft after draft, reminded me of what actually took place during some of our trips and is a constant source of encouragement. I couldn't have done it without all of you!

MY NAME IS BARRY and I have a problem. I like to t . . . t . . . t . . .

I look around the room at the expectant and encouraging faces. My face is breaking out in a cold sweat. I had avoided admitting my problem until now, but it's time to face up to it just as the others in this room had done before me. It's the moment of truth.

We're gathered in a hotel room in Miami, Florida. We have done this before—many times. The room is no different than others where we have congregated in the past. It's nicely air conditioned and big enough for all of us to fit in reasonably comfortably. It looks out onto a shaded street in Miami, with the startling bright Florida sunshine beating down through the Palmettos. It's about an hour's bus ride to the pier where tall, glistening cruise ships await their passengers to take them to idyllic destinations.

The room is labelled "standard." That means there are two double beds, one uncomfortable chair, and a small desk. The walls are construction white and, while there is no velvet Elvis, it looks like the pictures glumly hanging there were purchased at a local flea market . . . and not recently. The attendees are sprawled on the bed, on the one chair or standing. The carpet is badly worn. The television is a standard hotel issue forty-three inch that works when it feels like it. I look at the bed thinking that I wouldn't want to know what the Crime Scene Investigation unit would find if they shone their ultraviolet lights on the bed covers.

There are eight of us congregated here. To my immediate left is tall, slim, and statly Ed the Negotiator. He is the elder statesman of the group and has a full head of white hair, making those of us whose hair follicles seem to have retired long before we did insanely jealous. To his left is his wife, Carol, the Practical One. Her travel notes and accounts of expenses are legendary. To Carol's left is Cowboy Ron, the real-life cowboy who has an amazing talent for training horses. Next to Ron is his wife, Nurse Linda, who decided to follow her dream later in life and acquired the necessary qualifications to poke and prod people. There are two choices in life for those who like to poke and prod others, and, apparently, Linda didn't want to work in airport security. Even though her profession continually warns against it, Linda is the only smoker in the group and one of two with a severe coffee addiction.

Joke-a-Minute Jim sits next to Nurse Linda. I have learned that Jim has a joke for every occasion and, like most of us at this age who are able to hide our own Easter eggs, Jim occasionally has "senior moments" and recycles his jokes. But they are still funny because the rest of us can never remember the punch line. At times we would all be willing to swear on a tower of bibles that we had never heard it before, even though we probably had—on several occasions. On Jim's left is his better half, Short Brenda. She may be vertically challenged but she is also the gregarious one of the group, always friendly and smiling, and a lab and x-ray technician in the medical profession. Finally, closing the circle is my wife, Evelyn the Problem Solver, who always manages to think her way through a situation and come up with a solution. She is the second one addicted to coffee, a.k.a. the Travel Arranger, and the reason we're all here. As for me, well, I'm average.

I decide that the best way is to just blurt it out. Okay, here goes. I start again. This seems like the hardest thing I have ever had to say! I admit it. I like to t . . . t . . . t . . . TRAVEL!!

Yes, it's difficult to admit, but it's made easier by the fact that the statement is not entirely true. "Liking" to travel would imply an enjoyment of packing, waiting in lines at airports, going through Customs, checking in, checking out . . . It would be difficult for anyone to say with a straight face that they actually enjoy all that. American best-selling author Greg

I GUESS WE MISSED THE BOAT

Anderson said, "Focus on the journey, not the destination." A friend recently commented on Anderson's statement after being stranded in a Jamaican airport for hours. "Whoever said it's the journey, not the destination, deserves a shot in the head." I'm pretty sure Mr. Anderson was probably using "journey" in the context of an activity, not the mechanics of getting from one place to another. The reality is that most people don't like to *travel*. They like *being* at a new destination. But, in order to *be* at a new destination, you have to travel, so travel is what we do.

I'm thinking about this disparate group as we sit in the confines of our Miami hotel. We are a group of retirees who have had the good fortune to save enough money for travel. Or, we're working to supplement our pensions so we can travel. As we like to say, "We're spending the kids' inheritance and will leave them with any remaining bills." It's not that we are addicted to travel, but we have all worked long and hard to have the extra cash to travel as much as we do. We don't travel as much as some, but we travel more than others and we are very fortunate to be able to do that.

We're eight different people with different interests and backgrounds. But we all grew up on the Canadian prairies so the first initial sighting of earth that was less than flat was a moment of revelation for all of us. We had an inkling of how Christopher Columbus must have felt every additional minute that his three ships didn't fall into oblivion off the edge of the earth as he made his way across the ocean. We're all familiar with farming and some made it their careers. Surrounded by land as far as we could see in our formative years, our first view of a body of water larger than a small river transformed our eyes into saucers.

I have grown rather fond of the people I'm surrounded by in this standard room in Miami. I had to, I guess. With the exception of Evelyn, they are my in-laws and relatives by marriage. Evelyn is my wife of some forty-plus years. As for the in-laws, let me see if I can explain how this goes. Linda and Brenda are Evelyn's sisters. Ron is married to Linda. Carol is married to Ed, but she is also Ron's cousin. Ed is Evelyn's, Linda's, and

Brenda's cousin. Jim is married to Brenda; he and I aren't related to anyone in this group, except by marriage. As Jim puts it, he and I are only included because they needed someone to carry the luggage. They say the relationships just described are legal, even in the civilized world. I will take *their* word for it.

The family I married into has its share of characters. An uncle of the three sisters was a tall, gruff man who loved life. Aside from believing firmly that the moon landing was a hoax fabricated in Hollywood, he was a genuine, honest, hard-working farmer, as most farmers are. He loved to play practical jokes but he saved the best for the last. At his funeral, the hearse was blocked by a parked car at the church as the rest of the procession headed off to the cemetery for the burial. Apparently, the owner of the parked vehicle had chosen to ride with someone else and the funeral party waited at the cemetery . . . and waited . . . and waited. The sisters agreed that this was the uncle's last laugh as he somehow managed to orchestrate being late for his own burial.

Carol Burnett said, and the story about the uncle seems to illustrate, that comedy is equal to tragedy plus time. I have had the opportunity to travel with and without the group and there have been some events in my travels that seemed like minor tragedies when they happened, but time has managed to turn them into something better. I have probably forgotten most of what I once knew about our travels. I'm just happy that I'm not capable of forgetting what I didn't know. Not only do we work hard to be able to do the things we want to do when we're old enough to do them but we also work long and hard to earn the right to forget things.

Young people often comment on how lucky we are to be able to travel. Yeah, well, the unsympathetic side of me says, "Work for forty years, save a bit of money, and you will be *lucky* enough to travel, too!" In the meantime, this group that I'm with has reached the magical age when there are no longer kids to support and time belongs to us as we sit in this room reminiscing about the adventures and misadventures that haven't been forgotten. It's an opportunity to remind each other of some of the strange and wonderful things that have happened to us along the way.

Now that my admission of enjoying travel has been made, it's time to make a special presentation. Since our group has travelled quite a bit together, I thought it would be fun to have T-shirts made. It came to me as an epiphany in the shower. Maybe it's those positive ions that come out of the showerhead, but, for some reason, I do my best thinking in the shower. Whatever it is, I was trying to come up with a name that would combine everyone's last name into one fantastic group name.

Their surnames are Woods, Blight, and Dixon. It took some time, but I finally came up with one. I had mocked it up on the computer and I proudly present it to them during a lull in the discussion. There is good-natured laughter all around and the mockups are handed back to me. "Do you want the shirts? How many each?" The group achieves something that I haven't seen before and that I am unlikely to see ever again. They all immediately agree without beating the issue to death and they all reply in unison, like a well-rehearsed choral group, "NO!"

So the name shall go down in infamy, but it would have been something to see my six in-laws walking down the street in their black T-shirts, their names emblazoned on the back in bold white lettering. I can see it now: THE TRAVELLING WOBLIDIX.

IT ISN'T REALLY a tell-all session. We're simply in a holding pattern, as travellers often are. My finally admitting to liking to travel is an attempt to while away the time and entertain the others. Our suitcases are packed, and we're just killing time until we leave for the airport to catch our fights to our respective homes. Evelyn and I live in Ottawa, Canada, and the rest are from various towns in Manitoba, Canada. So, we do as many people our age do when they are killing time; we reminisce about the "old days."

The subject that we have most in common now is travel. Carol asks the question that stops everyone in their tracks. "Why do we travel? We could be using the money to buy things to make our everyday lives more comfortable. It isn't like we're all rich. We all had to save to be able to do this." A silence descends on the group for a few minutes. But any silence in this group is a token at best.

Ed the Negotiator says with a wistful look on his face, "I like to travel when I can get a deal. That always makes me feel good." There are understanding nods around the room. Not because the same is true for us, but we do understand that finding a deal would give him a warm and fuzzy feeling. He *is* the Negotiator, after all. Carol says it was a rhetorical question for her because she knows her answer: she really likes to taste new food in the various places we have been. Linda agrees, "As long as there are no red or green peppers."

Brenda adds, "And no corn."

Evelyn chimes in, "And make sure there are no olives on mine."

Hearing this and knowing that the food angle is going nowhere, Jim says, "Maybe it's the drinks that we go for."

Ron looks up from his Western novel, "As long as it's Budweiser."

"And no martinis." Evelyn again: "Especially, if they have olives."

Oh, boy! Finding consensus on this question among this group will be a challenge! But obviously, we like to travel or we wouldn't be here. I suggest that maybe it's because we like to see new things.

"Yes," says Brenda, "I love the gorgeous, fragrant, and peaceful gardens in the Caribbean."

Linda adds, "I like to see the ruins and ancient artifacts in Europe."

Evelyn points out that she likes the trees in Africa and the castles in Scotland.

Okay, well, these three *are* sisters. Ed jumps in to remind everyone that he likes a trip as long as he can get a good deal. Is that a groan I hear emanating from his wife, Carol? Why, yes, I think it might be.

It isn't that Ed is cheap. I would just say that he's fiscally responsible. And we can all learn from that, including some governments we all know and love. He knows the art of the deal and he's prepared to bargain when no one else will. He has also pointed out that now is the time, as the cost of travel-related health insurance starts to get out of hand as we age. There is a window of opportunity upon retirement when we are still healthy enough to travel and the insurance costs aren't outrageous. Of course, as we get older, both of those factors do a 180-degree turn. We're all looking through the window of opportunity right now as we sit together in Miami.

We're fortunate to be able to travel for pleasure. I'm quite sure that the genesis of travel was the search for food and basic necessities. It was a matter of survival, much like the wildebeest making their way across the plains of the Serengeti in their annual migration in search of grazing and water. Then, I suspect, as time went on, it became an opportunity to trade for supplies that weren't available locally. It wasn't necessarily for survival at that point, but it was used to make a better life. Now, we have progressed to the point where we travel for leisure; in some cases to relax and unwind.

But Evelyn sums it up best. "I think that travel is a learning experience. We travel to learn from others." It's true. We've been around the world. We've seen how fortunate we are to live where we do. We've also seen how happy others seem to be with so much less. We've marvelled at how humanity doesn't seem to have progressed much in many ways over the centuries. We've noted how religious differences have dominated the world for so many years and that the more things change, the more they remain the same. We've been worried about venturing out at night in Dar es Salaam, Tanzania, but realized that it isn't much different after dark than some areas of Chicago, Detroit, or any other major Western city.

Jim notes that we've all purchased souvenirs in various places to commemorate our having been there. Well, maybe except Ed who often negotiates items down to a point where the vendor can no longer sell them and he walks away empty handed. It's the hunt, not the catch for Ed. Jim reminds me of the "Rolex" watch my son brought me back from Southeast Asia. When I compared it with a real $14,000 Rolex, the only differences were the lighter weight of the gift watch, the smoother movement of the second hand of the real one and $13,990. The useful life of the two might have been different as well, although mine did last two years.

We've all taken countless pictures and bored our friends with them. We refuse to look at anyone else's photos until they've been narrowed down to two hundred or less so I guess we have to do the same. But it's the memories that last a lifetime. It's the knowledge we absorb that makes us better people. So someone among us has decided that we should relive these memories as we sit and wait. Everyone seems quite anxious to share their stories and to hear what each other's memories are. There are also moments of reflection as each of us is lost in our own thoughts about where their travels have taken them. This usually happens when the conversation narrows to two people and the rest of us drift off.

So this is the way we pass the time while we wait for our next flight on this sunny day in Miami. Let the stories begin!

3

WE CAN'T HELP but think of hotel rooms as we're holding our "meeting" in one. We all agree that we are never as comfortable on the road as we are at home. But some of the hotels we have stayed in have been beyond ridiculous.

When it comes to booking hotel rooms, I have a problem. My problem is that I'm an accountant by profession. Not that being an accountant is a bad thing. It has given me a great career, and I'm proud of my working life. But where it gets me into trouble, and I'm sure Ed has the same issue sometimes, is that my thought process starts with dollars and cents. If I can save $10 on a hotel room, I will. And that can mean the difference between sleep and no sleep.

There is any number of perils that can make for an incredibly long night. Paper-thin walls can, of course, lead to interesting times but not very restful sleep. As Jim points out, the rhythmic pounding of the headboard on the wall in the next room can be mildly entertaining for a few minutes, but when the gymnastic couple turns out to be in training for some kind of endurance award, the entertainment value wears thin very quickly. But once that sound is in your head, it's difficult to ignore. At least a ticking clock can be unplugged. It should be possible to cover your head with extra pillows, but good luck trying to find any. The front desk won't help. Something about what people do in the sanctity of their room is their business and all that. Yeah, well, what about the business of sleep?

Evelyn mentions that there are never enough pillows and rarely are there enough blankets. On a cold night, when the one thin sheet is covering the shivering occupants of the bed, little ice crystals start to form around the nostrils. It would be nice to add a blanket but there just aren't any. But hotel management have learned the art of avoiding lawsuits so the heating system cuts in just before the occupants reach a cryogenic state from which they could be revived in the next century. As the noise next door finally subsides, the heating system roars into life, with the sound of the horn of a cruise ship coming into port. It eventually docks and the heating system settles into the steady clickety-clack of the wheels of a freight train making its way across the plains.

When the heat does eventually come through, the one thin blanket is kicked to the floor and breathing becomes laboured as the air is slowly sucked out of the room. We might as well be floating in space without breathing apparatus as the atmosphere becomes a vacuum. The nostrils that were forming icicles only a few minutes before dry up and clamp shut. Mr. Sandman takes his job literally and drops sand into the mouths hanging open in the hopes of capturing the last vestiges of oxygen in the room. The sand won't be noticed until morning when the sleeper wakes to that gritty taste. Any attempt to open the windows to let in a little air is thwarted; they are sealed shut. Eventually the steady clickety-clack of the heating system lulls us into a light sleep until it suddenly reaches a crescendo and abruptly shuts down with a thud. We're wide awake again, but the heating system has done its duty for the time being and the cycle starts again. Of course, the same process applies in reverse when air conditioning is required.

It could not be considered a true cacophony of sound without adding the other noises suggested by Linda and Ron. Babies crying, people yelling and laughing in the halls, doors slamming, the crash of the ice machine next to the elevator all contribute to the decibel level. It's four a.m., the bed clothes are strewn everywhere by the occupants' thrashing about, trying to find a comfortable position on the rock-hard or too-soft bed. The heating system is off for the moment and the occupants are drifting off for what will, hopefully, be a few hours of much needed sleep. If they are unfortunate enough to be on the ground floor, further challenges emerge out of the dark: a truck will inevitably start up outside. On a cold morning, it will sit and idle for forty minutes as it warms up. Then ,with a crash of gears, it will roar off. Will the night never end? As someone so aptly pointed out, it's possible to sleep like a baby in a hotel room: sleep, wake up, cry . . . sleep, wake up, cry . . .

Might as well get up and have a shower. The mirror reflects back an image of a scarecrow with hair sticking up at all angles, the result of alternating between sweltering and freezing during the night. But there is the continental breakfast to look forward to. It might take a while to figure out the shower as it has one of an infinite number of fixtures found in hotel rooms to keep us off balance. Once the deciphering is done, it's time to allow the shower to get us ready for a brand new day.

Ouch! It's too hot.

Step back out of the stream and adjust the tap. That's better!

Whoa, now it's freezing!

Okay, I'm awake.

One more peek in the mirror confirms it. The hair has been smoothed back to normal but the eyes are like pie plates, so I must be awake.

Brenda mentions that it's little wonder the hotel residents can be seen trudging silently toward the continental breakfast as if on autopilot, bags drooping beneath their eyes. After a night of everything a hotel room has to offer, it's a wonder that anyone is upright. But there is the "free" continental breakfast to prepare us for the day ahead. Let's see, today shall we have rubber eggs and burned toast with our coffee swill? Nope, cereal and orange juice should be fine.

The tired and hungry travellers return to their room to retrieve their belongings. The key card is inserted into the reader on the door and the light remains red. Try it again. Still red. Back down to the lobby to have the key card reprogrammed as it somehow became demagnetized in your pocket. Finally in the room and it's time to send an email message to your loved ones to tell them everything is fine and you wish they were there with you (after all, why should you be suffering alone) but you can't get a signal.

Defeated, weary, and perhaps a little irrational and emotional, it's time to move on to the next hotel.

We should consider ourselves fortunate in North America. Our two trips to Africa have proven that hotel rooms can be even worse as we've had to deal with baboons on the roof, electricity that is intermittent at best, and hot water that is only available for short periods of time each day, not to mention the potential of crawly things as co-occupants.

We're having fun with this, of course, because it's doubtful that all of it will happen to anyone on one eventful trip, but everything we have discussed has happened to all of us at one time or another. It has taken me a long time to learn one valuable lesson. It doesn't pay to save $10 on a hotel room. A good night's sleep is priceless. But once an accountant, always an accountant, so I hope I can remember this maxim on future trips.

4

EVERYONE IN THIS GROUP that is sharing a laugh in Miami grew up in small towns on the Canadian prairies . . . a place normally associated with cold and mosquitoes, but also with abundant sunshine, open spaces, and fresh air. It's a different life growing up in a small town. There's an old saying that the benefit of living in a small town is that if you don't know what you're doing, someone else will. No truer words were spoken!

While the group is discussing various issues and undoubtedly solving most of the world's problems, my thoughts turn to life in the small town I grew up in. Once on a visit, I had borrowed my brother's car on a cold, frosty winter day and parked it outside my mom's house. The weather could be described in meteorological terms as "fresh." The car seemed happy enough sitting there huddled in the cold with its windows covered in ice, but I had errands to run. The car grumbled bitterly when I turned the key. Slowly, the engine turned over and, finally, after spluttering a few times and with obvious displeasure, it barked into life. It really didn't seem to want to be bothered. It preferred to wait out the cold, hoping there were better days ahead. So I went into the house while it warmed up. Little did I know it was quietly plotting its revenge.

When I thought the car might be warm enough to sit in reasonably comfortably, I donned my cold weather attire of a hooded winter coat, accessorized by a toque, scarf, snow boots, and gloves, and left the house. The car was sitting there idling, angry vapours emanating from its exhaust. "Oh, come on, get over it," I thought. There was no remote start or keyless entry in those days. The car doors had to be unlocked and the car had to be started with a key. I know this may come as a shock to some.

With my mind thoroughly distracted by the errands I had to run, I braved the elements long enough to remove the glove from my left hand to retrieve the keys from my coat pocket so I could unlock the car. Not in that one. As I continued walking, my breath clearly visible, I put my glove back on, removed the one on my right hand and checked the pocket on the other side. Not there either. Maybe I left them in the house. When I got to the car, I could see what had happened through the now semi-frosted windows. The keys were in the car . . . and the car was locked! I could see them in the ignition. In my completely distracted state, I had forgotten about starting the car earlier. The engine seemed to pick up its rhythm as if it was humming with malicious pleasure, and the vapours from the exhaust appeared to clear. I am sure if it could have, the grill would have wrinkled into a lopsided grin.

I called my nephew who came to the rescue and had the door open in about a minute. I have wondered to this day how he did that; it may help explain the car collection he had. Everyone in the room knows I'm just kidding. They all know my nephew and they're well aware that he's not one to be stealing cars. But the interesting thing about all this, aside from the embarrassment of having done something that stupid, was that immediately after the car door was open, I got in and drove down to the local store. When I walked in, the owner looked at me and said, "So, I hear you locked your keys in the car."

How does that happen in a small town? Does the news travel in the air to be distributed to everyone within a certain radius by the currents, like an exuberant paperboy hurling the newspaper at the door? I went directly downtown; my nephew didn't go anywhere close to the store, and I didn't see any smoke signals. It's one of those mysteries that shall forever remain unsolved.

It was beyond cold the day I locked my keys in the car, and the conversation, as it invariably does on our trips, turns to the depth of cold we were all experiencing in our respective communities when we left home. We Canadians never have a lack of subjects to talk about. The weather is good filler for any conversation. "Do you remember the snow of '54?" "What about that year the hailstones were as big as softballs?" Surprisingly, the cold is always discussed briefly; we rarely dwell on it in any detail because it's just something that happens every winter and Canadians deal with it. And the way many people deal with it is to escape to warmer climes for a break. It isn't that we dislike the cold. There are things to do in the winter. We can skate, ski, play hockey, curl, shovel snow, get stuck in the snow with our cars, and freeze our asses off. Okay, maybe we do dislike the cold a little.

Even in a cold country like Canada there are levels of cold. I thought of the four months it felt like I spent in Churchill, Manitoba, in the mid-seventies. Churchill is on the shores of the Hudson Bay and it's a lovely town . . . for some. You either love it or you don't. I wasn't particularly enamored with it during the ten days I was actually there. I thought I would let the group in on the experience I had in this converging point in northern Manitoba that is situated with boreal forest to the south, the Arctic tundra to the northwest, and the Hudson Bay to the north and east. I thought it was time to bring the cold out of the closet, so to speak, so I launched into my tale of the temperature.

It's not the town of Churchill that I dislike and I certainly can't comment on what it's like now since I haven't been back since the early seventies. I do know it's now known as the "Polar Bear Capital of the World." The people were arguably some of the friendliest on the planet. What I disliked about the town is the weather. For those who may not have surmised it by now, Churchill is cold. How cold is it, you may ask? Well, according to Wikipedia, Churchill has a subarctic climate and its winters are "colder than a location at a latitude of 58 degrees north should warrant, given its coastal location. Prevailing northerly winds from the North Pole jet across the frozen bay and chill it to a −26.7°C (−16.1°F) January average. Juneau, Alaska, by contrast, is also located at 58 degrees north but its January average temperature is a full 23.2°C (41.8°F) warmer than Churchill's." That would make Churchill very cold indeed!

Our eldest son, Trevor, has moved to a much warmer city than the one he grew up in and he now has a three-stage description of the temperature in our house in the winter. We don't keep our house cold, but the thermostat is set at a temperature that we have become accustomed to. He refers to the first stage as simply, "I can see my breath!" The second stage is, "Museum Cold." The third stage is, "Oh, my God, I can't feel my extremities!" I think he doth exaggerate, but Churchill clearly qualifies for stage three!

I was a student with a firm of chartered accountants in the seventies and, for some reason, I was seconded to work with an accountant in Churchill in January. January!!?? This wasn't any ordinary January either, with the bone-numbing cold described in Wikipedia. No, this was much, much worse! I have often searched my memory banks to try to figure out what I did wrong to warrant that kind of punishment and I haven't come up with any logical explanation. I'm pretty sure I wasn't asked if I wanted to go. However, having a bit of a sense of adventure, I probably looked forward to it.

Having been born and raised on a farm in rural Manitoba, I knew how to dress for the cold weather. Being bundled up so that any kind of movement was nearly impossible was not uncommon in the winter. Exposed skin was unheard of. However, in 1967 I moved to the big city of Winnipeg at the tender and know-it-all age of eighteen, and it became unfashionable to wear layers of clothing in the winter. It was considered cool to be cold, if you know what I mean. So, an overcoat and gloves became the fashion statement in Winnipeg.

For some inexplicable reason, I forgot my roots and carried that attitude with me to the frozen north, so an overcoat and gloves were what I was wearing when I stepped off the plane in Churchill. I was hit with a blast of frigid arctic air that immediately brought me to tears and threatened to freeze my eyes permanently shut. I had to concentrate to ensure that the downward movement of my blink didn't last a microsecond too long or my eyes would have been cemented in that position until I left for home. The thought of being led onto the plane with my eyes frozen shut did not endear the north to me. The first intake of air made my teeth ache and left icicles in my lungs . . . or so it seemed. Streams of vapour wafted past my head every time I exhaled as little puffy clouds accompanied every breath.

"Welcome to Churchill," my greeter said with a hint of sarcasm in his voice as he observed my attire while standing at the bottom of the steps leading from the aircraft. No problem with standing on the tarmac in those days! It was a simpler time. Through my tear-stained and frosted eyes I could barely make out a bundle under his arm, which turned out to be a gigantic parka and mitts that he had brought for me. These people are not only friendly, they are thoughtful!

There were a few harbingers of things to come that day. For those of you who haven't been lucky enough to experience it, if it's cold enough, there is an unmistakable sound that you make as you walk in the frigid air on the frozen ground. It's a crunching sound, and, if everything is quiet around you, it's like tiny gunshots going off every time you take a step. It was like that. When we reached the car, which had been left running, we drove through the frigid afternoon air to my home for the next few days. The tires crunched on the frozen tundra, complaining at the insult of being forced to turn on a day like that. Like a union demonstrating against the latest wage freeze, they protested loudly and continuously. Their form of protest was to demonstrate they were less than round as we bumped and thumped on our way to the destination. Much like the car with its keys locked inside, this one didn't want to move either. It knew where it *wanted* to be and it certainly wasn't outside. It creaked, it moaned, it groaned. There was probably a nice, toasty (relatively speaking) garage waiting for it somewhere.

As we made our way along the road, in spite of the protests of the vehicle, I learned that there were two hotels on the main street. They were across from each other and one was good, the other not so much. Fortunately, I had been booked into the "good" hotel. I made my way to my room, found the door was ajar and walked in. After throwing my suitcase on the bed, I opened the bathroom door and found my second greeter to Churchill. However, this one didn't offer me a welcome. He couldn't. In fact, the dishevelled gentleman lying motionless in "my" bathtub was apparently sleeping off an eventful evening. When I went back to the front desk to advise them of the situation, they were apologetic, but knew exactly who it was. Apparently, it was a normal occurrence. In fact, they were so calm about the situation I thought they could have hung the sleeping intruder up as a sign advertising the comforts of their establishment. I was given another room.

The week was filled with working, often in my room, going for dinner and being entertained by something that was going on outside. Occasionally, the entertainment moved inside. One night, I went with my two colleagues for a beer in the "good" hotel where we were staying before retiring for the night. We were sitting quietly talking among ourselves when I felt a pair of arms draped around my neck, two rather large breasts plastered against my back, and a stale-beer-scented female voice whispering breathlessly in my ear. "Give me your room number." I looked at my comrades who were grinning from ear to ear, obviously thrilled that it was not happening to them.

I peered around her large left breast as far as I could given the proximity of her mouth to my ear. The first thing I saw was a toothless grin mostly obscured by long unkempt hair. I mumbled something about being married and not interested, while I could hear my two "friends" stifling bursts of laughter. A discussion ensued; my ear was getting damper and my protestations were becoming louder when finally she stood up and said, "Never mind, my boyfriend is over there anyway." She finally withdrew her arms and her breasts and staggered back to her companion who was rather large and slumped over, hugging the table to make sure it didn't somehow get away from him. We quickly got up and left as we had visions of him waking up like a hungry bear out of hibernation.

Unimaginably, it became colder as the wind increased and a storm blew in. It was well below –80 degrees Fahrenheit when the force of the wind was combined with the outside temperature (known to us cold weather inhabitants as wind chill) and everything except the emergency skidoos stopped moving. I'm sure many of you grew up in a cold climate and your mothers told you never to stick your tongue on a metal object. I am also sure many of you immediately did it. Well, in Churchill, had we been able to see through the blizzard, I'm sure we would have seen plenty of young people, who didn't listen to their mothers either, stuck by the tongue to the various metal objects around town. That would probably be a better deterrent than warning signs anyway!

I continued to work indoors but the frost building up on the inside walls led to poor working conditions. Working in a parka and trying to hold a pencil with mitts was not ideal. When I related this story to the group, I remarked, "Fortunately, my computer didn't freeze," just testing to see if they are paying attention! Ed picks up on it right away. "Are you sure there were computers in those days?" Good catch!

The polar bears that are now a popular tourist attraction were a nuisance at that time and so the local Game and Fish people were painting red circles on their butts and flying them further north. The red circles allowed for tracking the bears and popular legend had it that they would make it back to Churchill before the airplanes. I only have one question. Why would they want to?

Since we couldn't go outside for fear our frozen bodies would not be discovered until summer, I watched Canada's number one religious show on Saturday night, *Hockey Night in Canada*. It had been a week since I had arrived in Churchill. Oddly, it was the same teams playing as the game I had watched at home the previous Saturday and they seemed to be scoring at the same time in the game. Hold on a second! *It's the same game*!! I later found out that tapes (this was the mid-seventies, remember) were being flown in and the game was televised locally the following weekend.

Earlier in the day, foreshadowing the hockey game, a fight had broken out on the street. There were some good punches thrown and it was a pretty even fight. A bottle of something had broken on the sidewalk and that seemed to be what led to the altercation. I can only assume that it would be more of the same that evening in the "bad" hotel across the street, but it would more likely be the *men* fighting this time.

It was definitely an experience that I will never forget. Churchill is a very popular tourist destination now, and there are many people who told me when I was there that they would never live anywhere else. It has camaraderie. People are brought together by the common element of extreme cold. People actually make eye contact and talk to their neighbours. Maybe they know too much about their neighbours, but there is friendliness in a small town that is unmatched in the city. People feel safe and secure. You can always find someone you know when you go for coffee.

I grew up in a small town so it wasn't as if I was experiencing something entirely new. But it was a great experience to see people dealing with extreme conditions with smiles on their faces. Like any town or city, the downtown area often does not say everything there is to say about a community. I would like to go back someday *in the summer* to see the best side of Churchill. In the meantime, as Friedrich Nietzsche apparently said, that which didn't kill me made me stronger. He forgot to add that it would also prepare me for future travel experiences.

5

ANYONE LISTENING in on our conversation, and especially if they have not experienced the cold and snow for long periods at a time, may still wonder why we would not love every minute of it. There is a certain romanticism about snow, especially when viewed from thousands of miles away in a continuously hot climate. The snow is so pristine. It's magical to be able to actually see your breath. It's romantic to sit in front of a roaring, crackling fire on a cold day, drinking cocoa and watching the snowflakes drift down outside. Linda points out that she just read an article about a recent survey indicating that Canadians have less fun than, well, almost anyone on the planet. I think it depends on the definition of fun. There are so many exciting activities to do outdoors, right?

Well, right! It was with that thought in mind that our friends Don and Janet and their two daughters rented a house with Evelyn, our boys, and me at Jay Peak, Vermont, for a winter ski vacation. Jay Peak lies just to the south of the Canada–U.S. border and is therefore a popular skiing and recreation destination for both Canadians and Americans. At about 3,450 feet, it offers some great skiing with lots of trails and great snow. In fact, legend has it that Jay Peak gets almost twice as much snow as any other slope in the area. And to top it all off, the Jay Peak restaurant offers the heart attack–inducing combination of French-fried potato chips, cheese curds, and gravy, called poutine, a favourite dish among French Canadians. You know those little things that dam up your arteries? They *love* to see poutine coming. You haven't lived, and possibly died, if you haven't eaten poutine! Jay Peak was clearly the perfect place for the two families to go for a vacation.

The house we rented was large and offered some wonderful

space for the eight of us. My friend Don and I couldn't wait to get our respective daughters and sons out on the slopes. There's nothing like the scene of snow hanging on the branches of green pine and cedar trees like icing dripping off a cake. There is that first sharp intake of air as we exited the warmth of our cozy accommodation to the c-c-c-cold of the outdoors. In contrast to my trip to Churchill, though, the air was cold but not enough to freeze your lungs solid at impact. It's times like these I know why we travel!

We were all decked out in our bulky ski parkas and pants, toques to cover our ears and to keep whatever warmth we had in our heads from escaping, and warm gloves. To this we had to add the rented ski equipment, consisting of enormous heavy boots that we clomped around in like astronauts on the moon but without the bounce. Getting the rental gear is akin to sharing locker space at the gym. It can be done but you have to be tolerant of your neighbour. At least with the ski rental, your closest neighbour isn't naked!

We were sweating from the exertion of the rental experience as we headed off for a lesson. The only one who had skied before was Don so our two boys, Trevor and Chris, and I thought we should have some idea what we were doing before actually launching ourselves downhill. Following the lesson, we were fully prepared to tackle the bunny slope, which is a nice, gentle hill designed for beginners. It was great fun skiing with the boys and Don and his girls. Don took off on a few occasions and tried more adventurous slopes, but I was happy just cruising up and down the bunny slope with the kids.

But, of course, humans have this failing of "needing" more. It's foot-itis in boating where the boater always "needs" a bigger boat. Golfers have club-itis, where they always "need" better clubs or car racers with their "need" for more speed. Actresses "need" bigger, ummm ... assets. Well, you get the picture. A skier "needs" higher and faster hills. So it was that we all ventured out to the intermediate slope a couple of days into our vacation.

Inevitably, there is a chair lift to get to the starting point, and the first challenge is exiting gracefully from the chair. There are three options. The first is to raise your butt off the lift, putting your weight on your skis and letting the chair gently propel you toward your departure point. The second is to wait a little too long and get ejected awkwardly, often into a face-down position in the snow, as the lift makes its turn back down the mountain. The third is to sit paralyzed in the chair as it makes its turn, forcing the lift operator to stop the entire operation and leaving a number of frustrated skiers hovering in the air with their legs dangling and ready to strangle you for making them wait an extra minute or two. Skiers can be so rude!

Don and his two girls and our two boys easily accomplished the first extraction. Mine was more along the lines of the second option. I was gently ejected toward the slope, but I'm sure I looked like an inebriated flamingo trying to maintain its balance on one leg. However, it was a minor embarrassment compared to what it could have been and it was on to bigger challenges.

The next obstacle was the slope itself. The view from our vantage point was breathtaking and well worth the awkward exit from the chair! The aforementioned picture of the snow hanging from the trees was magnified exponentially at this height, and the view in the distance of other snow-capped peaks was truly startling. I could have stayed there all day . . . and you know what? I really wanted to. Looking down the trail, I wasn't sure I was ready for this. However, there is a maxim that I learned when I climbed Mount Kilimanjaro later on and it applies here. Going up is optional. Coming down is mandatory.

Finally, I worked up the courage to begin the run. And it was everything I dreamed it would be. Watching the kids with their new-found knowledge and lack of inhibition was inspiration enough for me to push off. The feeling of the wind on my face and the freedom of gliding along the snow on a pair of skis was well worth the effort. The sound of the skis hissing on the fresh snow was exhilarating! There was nothing as sweet as the image in the mind's eye of my elegant form as I imagined myself sluicing down the hill with the speed and grace of a downhill racer on his way to the podium to accept his medal at the end of his run. It had to be done again and again.

The best run in skiing keeps bringing you back, apparently. Just like in golf, when you hit the perfect shot and it drags you back. You never play golf badly enough to quit. You never ski badly enough to quit. You know you can duplicate it or even do it better and you have to go back. Or do you? Well, my friends, I found out it was possible to have a run that was bad enough to make me want to quit. My last run at Jay Peak was very nearly that.

We had all been up and down a few times and our confidence was growing with every run. I was standing at the top of the trail feeling pretty good about things and pushed off. I gently moved my knees and body in unison, fully in control of the run. The wind was blowing in my face and there was the rush of scoring a goal, hitting a home run, hitting that perfect golf shot to within six inches of the pin. I was conquering my little section of the mountain as the trees and rocks swept by to my left and right. Okay, maybe "swept" is a slight exaggeration as a couple of times some six-year-old girls skied by me with the ease of the great downhill racer I had imagined myself to be moments before, but overall it was a great feeling.

As I crested the first of two hills, there standing in front of me was a group of teenagers, right in the middle of the run. Apparently, one had fallen and the others had all congregated to make sure she was okay. I had two choices. The first was to plow through them, and, while it flashed through my mind as the best option for me, the collateral damage would have been too great. I did the next best thing. I bailed out, and the subsequent crash was nothing short of spectacular. My glasses went one way. One ski went another. My legs did something similar. My hearing was still good as I could hear the teenagers giggling as I cartwheeled past. I noticed they didn't seem to be speaking English, but giggling seems to be universal. Don, who had been skiing nearby, came up to make sure I was alive and well and in complete control of my extremities and faculties. My extremities all checked out but my faculties had taken a bit of a hit. He retrieved my loose ski and helped me navigate to the bottom on very wobbly legs. After he was sure I was more or less intact,

I could hear him chuckle a little as he recalled the sight of me tumbling down the mountain.

As we relaxed at the house that night, Don came up with the perfect solution to my aches and pains. A hot bath and a giant glass of whiskey with a hint of ice did the trick. I slept very well and spent the rest of the week nursing my bruises and relaxing in the chalet with the wives. I can't say that was the only reason I gave up my skiing career. Our sons and I did ski a couple of times after that, but every time we did, it was icy and a little too treacherous for my liking. Trevor has also given up the sport. I'm happy to report that Chris is actively pursuing skiing along with his young daughter, who I'm sure will be racing by old guys on the mountain around her sixth birthday.

All I can say is I love my new snowshoes!

6

SO WE'VE COLLECTIVELY stumbled across another good reason we like to travel. To escape the cold! Most of our travel has occurred in the winter for that very reason. The thought of a cruise to Alaska has been raised but that would only make sense if we go in the summer. There doesn't appear to be much enthusiasm for that.

Although we've only been sitting here a few minutes, Nurse Linda, who is in her flowered top and blue jeans, is starting to get a little fidgety. Her face is slightly creased, perhaps from years of smoking, but her hair remains a brown colour. Her fidgeting can mean one of three things. It's time for a coffee or it's time for some "fresh" air or it's time for both. The answer quickly comes clear as she grabs her smokes off the bed and heads out into the Florida sunshine. "Be right back," she says as she makes her way to the door, cigarette pack clutched firmly in her hand.

The conversation veers off in a few different directions again. There has been enough talk about cold weather so the conversation turns to the drought across some areas of North America in the summer, and Jim mentions it was so dry that the trees were whistling for the dogs. On that note, my mind drifts off again. All this talk about travel has started me thinking about the first major form of transportation that I think we all experienced.

We've all travelled on various forms of conveyance. We've travelled by car, plane, and ship. We've experienced resort-style living. But probably the first mode of travel for all of us who grew up in the country was the mother of all mass travel — the bus. Well, maybe the first conveyance for some of them was by horse-drawn sleigh, but no one seems to be interested in talking about that.

I GUESS WE MISSED THE BOAT

I have mixed feelings about buses. The ones that carry us now on bus tours are comfortable, air conditioned, relatively quiet behemoths. It's like riding in a giant limousine and I will be happy to start that conversation later on if someone else doesn't. The reason for my mixed feelings about buses stems from the fact that I have taken approximately sixteen thousand bus rides in my life. Who rides the bus sixteen thousand times, you might ask? Well, if you are a lifer on the transit system, you can probably make the same claim. Let's do the math. I started riding a school bus when I was six years old and did so for twelve years. So, let's see, that's about forty-eight hundred bus rides. I rode the bus for about twenty-five of my working years. That's another eleven thousand bus rides. I think I'm being conservative in my estimates and I can say this: it's a lot of mind- and butt-numbing bus rides.

School buses are not the giant limos I just described. The ones we rode in varied in size from vans to larger, yellow, barely functional vehicles. In my high school years, we were segregated, with the girls in one and the boys in the other. In high school, we had a trip of about eighteen miles to the school with a straight stretch of four miles leading into our hometown. On more than one occasion, one of the more unruly male students would end up walking at least part of the four miles into town.

Behaviour that warranted ejection from the bus could be anything from badmouthing the driver or a fist fight to swearing to cutting a hose leading on the inside of the bus from the front to the back. That is what one of my classmates did! I'm not sure what purpose the liquid that dribbled out of the hose served, but it earned the perpetrator a nice long walk on a cold day. We grew up tough on the prairies!

Riding the school bus was like a first bike with training wheels, but eventually the support was removed and it evolved into riding the city bus. While graduation from school to university and eventually to a job is something to look forward to, graduating from a school bus to a city bus is not necessarily a promotion. Often crammed from front to back and driven by a grouchy driver, they were incredibly uncomfortable, noisy, and often contributed to global warming as they belched clouds of black smoke into the atmosphere. A "good morning" to the driver upon getting on the bus would usually earn an unintelligible response that sounded something like, "Gmmmph."

While getting a seat was like hitting the jackpot, there was always the danger of being knocked unconscious by a student's backpack as the kids crowded off the bus. While I never actually witnessed it, I often wondered if the bus driver occasionally found two or three people slumped over unconscious at the end of the route, with the imprint of a backpack in their heads. It's the bus rider's version of the *Hunger Games*!

Then there is another problem. As I describe the situation, Jim eloquently refers to it as the problem of "armpits and assholes." Jim looks a little like Mr. Howell from *Gilligan's Island*. He has aged well; his hair is thinning a bit, and glasses adorn his weathered face. He has a joke for every occasion. He loves to jab Linda about her smoking and he has been known to move to the far end of the line if the eight of us are walking outside and Nurse Linda is "nursing" a cigarette. Any grumpiness is usually forgiven as the rest of us are usually busy groaning over his latest one-liner.

His graphic description of the challenge on the bus brings me back to my story. Managing to score a seat at the end of a long day at work can be a mixed blessing. This applies to everyone, but it must be especially so for anyone who has been on their feet all day. Passengers are jammed shoulder to shoulder as the bus jounces along on its route and more and more people shove their way onboard as it makes its way from the downtown core toward the suburbs. There is a rhythm to bus riding as everyone automatically leans back as the bus lurches forward and then everyone leans forward as the bus screeches to an abrupt halt at its next stop. The level of mumbling increases as the bus driver suddenly discovers an intelligible language and yells, "Further back, please." It is legally unwise to get any closer to your bus neighbour, whether you would like to or not. It is hot outside and hotter still inside the bus.

I GUESS WE MISSED THE BOAT

You're tired and grouchy when, suddenly, the seat beside you opens up. You cast a quick look around, shove the pregnant lady in front of you out of the way, and slide into the seat beside the largest person on the bus. Eureka! In spite of the fact you only have one butt cheek resting on the seat and your head is in that danger zone where a shot from flailing backpacks and the ensuing loss of consciousness is imminent, it feels like you have won the lottery. But wait a minute, what's that smell? You look up and there is someone's wet armpit hanging just above your head as they hold on for dear life. You look slightly to your left and there is someone's butt about six inches from your face. As you swing your gaze forward, your eyes burn a little; there is another person's crotch even closer. I don't even want to talk about the people wearing Depends®. You slowly get up with a smile and an apology and offer your seat to the pregnant lady.

Riding into the downtown core from the suburbs was usually less crowded and I occasionally had someone to talk to, making the ride that much more pleasant. But there were many times when I didn't have anyone to talk to and the ride became repetitive and boring. Admittedly, there are various ways to keep one's mind occupied. For example, there are people to watch; probably every human failing (and virtue) is on display at one time or another in the small village that occupies the bus. It is a virtual microcosm of humanity. There are people of all shapes and sizes. People fall in love, people fall out of love, people leave things behind, people die, babies are born . . . There are even occasional acts of kindness! If everyone was on the bus for just a little longer, it might even be possible to elect a mayor and council and give your bus village a name.

For me, one of the most obnoxious situations is when my seatmate falls asleep on my shoulder. However, if I am on the side of the seat next to the window and, as a regular commuter, I know the corners the bus will be taking. A little shove timed just right as you are turning the corner will jettison your sleeping companion into the aisle. The technique is especially effective in the winter. Those who are more concerned with warmth than appearance will throw fashion to the winds and don brightly coloured nylon coats that make their arms hang almost straight out, forced that way by the sheer bulk of their apparel. If they're also wearing ski pants, you've hit the jackpot.

The air is permeated with a swishing noise as people walk from one location to another with their arms rubbing against the sides of their coats. Brenda elaborates: "The noise is like the one that corduroy pants used to make when you walked, only it's a softer sound. Man, I hated those pants!" Exactly! While the jackets are warm, they can also be slippery on a vinyl seat, and it's much easier to land your unsuspecting neighbour on the floor. They will get up with a sheepish grin, and you will have satisfied yourself *and* entertained the other residents of your bus village.

I found another way to relieve the boredom. I tried to will people into doing things. I would stare at the back of their heads and say under my breath things like, "get off at the next stop" or "scratch your left ear." I did this time after time on the bus. I thought if I could learn mind control, work would never be the same. I could visualize people wandering around the office like the "Walking Dead," getting my coffee or even doing my work for me with a benign smile on their faces. After eight hours straight without smoke, coffee, or lunch break, they would wonder at the end of the day why they were simultaneously hungry, exhausted, and stuffing three cigarettes between their lips at once. Who knows, if I could perfect it, I might even have a shot at world peace!

I really thought I was getting close one day when I was trying to will someone to get off the bus. He was a well-dressed man, sitting quietly in his seat staring vacantly straight ahead. He had that mindless, glassy-eyed zombie look that most commuters adopt shortly after settling in for the ride. I knew that he was a perfect subject. I could tell that his mind was blank. I stared at the back of his head, silently transmitting my message over and over, "You will disembark at the mall." Before we got to the stop, I could see him lifting his briefcase. I smiled to myself but I didn't want to break the trance so I kept staring and sending my message. As the bus slowed down, he got up and moved to the door. I knew I had him in my power. I looked away, not wanting him to pick up on my controlling stare. I expected him to sit down again, but he didn't. The bus stopped and he got off! *Oh my God*! I did it! I actually convinced him to get off the bus!

I looked out and watched him, knowing that he would be bewildered at why he was on the sidewalk at *that* time of the day in *that* part of town. But he wasn't bewildered. He simply walked toward the mall, as if he belonged there. Wait a minute! When he turned around and waved just before entering the building, I realized he *did* belong there. He was my neighbour . . . a retail clerk who works in the building. He was probably trying to get my attention as he got off the bus, but I didn't notice because I was concentrating so hard to control him.

Sigh! Back to the amateur mind control drawing board. The title of Jedi Warrior still eludes me. I never did perfect it . . . at least not to my knowledge. If someone ever did, it would be an incredibly powerful weapon.

I have told the story to Trevor and Chris in the hopes that they will someday be able to perfect the technique and use it for good. But they never ride the bus so they are not enclosed with potential subjects long enough to work their will on the back of anyone's head! Maybe the technique will be passed on to our grandchildren.

I have retired from the mind control game and moved on to other modes of transportation. In spite of the adventures and misadventures on the school and city buses, it was an enjoyable part of my life and obviously worth a few stories. There is one thing I don't miss. I still have a monthly bus pass from 1985 that cost $40. To have the right to be a member of the bus village twenty-seven years later, that same pass will cost $116, an increase of almost 300 percent! Ah, even the bus village is not immune from inflation.

But travelling on school and city buses was great experience for graduating to the Master of all buses, the luxury cruise liners of the highways. We were off to visit faraway places . . . with the in-laws!

7

JIM DECIDES THAT we have gone long enough without hearing a joke (what has it been . . . fifteen minutes?). He tells us that there were three older women talking at home the other day. According to Jim, one said, "I forget everything. When I stand in front of the refrigerator with a jar of pickles, I can't remember whether I am getting them out or putting them away." The second one says, "I know what you mean. I find myself on the stairs sometimes not knowing whether I'm going up or down." The third one says, "I'm happy I don't have that problem. Knock on wood." She raps three times on the table and says, "I wonder who's at the door? I'll get it."

We tried to ignore the myth that bus tours are for the old and forgetful when we decided to try one in Scotland, and the conversation logically follows from the school bus to the bus limos. We don't consider ourselves old, even though we're all over sixty. It's funny how our perspective about the word "old" changes as we age! Anyway, the sisters all agree that they wanted to tour Scotland to fulfill a dream their father had had and because there would be eight of us travelling together, there was no better way to do it than by bus.

Organized bus tours don't take place on city or school buses. These are the Rolls Royce of buses, with comfortable seating, excellent suspension, and very experienced and capable drivers and guides. The drivers can manoeuvre their giant charges through the narrowest of streets, sometimes having to fold in the side mirrors to be able to squeeze through.

The guides are incredibly friendly and knowledgeable but they also know when it's time to stop talking and let everyone catch their breath. When taking a specialized tour, we were often joined by a guide who was more familiar with the area.

I GUESS WE MISSED THE BOAT

One gentleman boarded the bus at one location, wearing the traditional kilt. He decided to answer the unasked question before anyone in the bus raised it. He said, "You know, I'm often asked if anything is worn under this kilt." Everyone on the bus, and especially the women I'm guessing, waited with anticipation for the answer. Is he going to tell us? Please don't tell me he's going to *show* us! Finally, he said, "I just want you to know that everything under the kilt is in good working order."

The bus is huge but it's equipped to be lowered by the driver to make it easier for people to board. In fact, it's so big we were told that the Royal Air Force uses tourist buses to simulate army tanks and locks onto them with their radar as they are passing through northern Scotland. I'm still not sure if that story was to shake up the tourists, but we were happy when we emerged from the target zone before some overzealous pilot reduced our comfortable, luxurious ride into a smoldering heap of charred metal.

The tour starts with a "let's get acquainted party" and ends with a "let's stay in touch" party. Because we're such a large group, we quickly become known among the other passengers. It's especially true because of the mix of characters we have with us. Ron attracts people everywhere he goes and the rest of us are pretty easy to get along with. We quickly become known as the "The Canadians." I'm sure it's not because any of us ever say, "eh." We probably would have been even more noticeable if the others had agreed to the "TRAVELLING WOBLIDIX" T-shirts, but alas, that idea has been forever shelved.

Everything on a bus tour is managed so that we all get to know each other a little and the time seems to race by. And similar to the city bus, the tour bus quickly becomes a microcosm of humanity. Every day, couples sharing seats are requested to move two seats in a clockwise rotation so those on one side move further back and those on the other side move two seats forward. The result is that every day you are sitting across the aisle from someone different. Everyone ends up chatting to everyone else and getting to know a little about them. In theory it works great.

Friendships are made, and by the same token, we quickly become aware of the fellow traveller that we hope doesn't end up across the aisle from us. There was one young man who spoke one hundred miles an hour with a speech impediment and strong accent that no one could understand. Nice enough fellow, but it wears a person out constantly straining to understand or asking him to repeat what he just said . . . more than once. If you resort to smiling and nodding, you'll often attract a perplexed look when the up and down nod should have been the sideways version. Ed points out that he had the misfortune of losing the lottery one day, but we all noticed he had done an amazing job of nodding his head in the right direction at the right times. It may have been because he can't hear that well anyway so he was lip reading.

Everyone agrees that it was rare to see Ed lose the lottery. In fact, it generated a few chuckles when he reminded us. I mention that my luck was completely the opposite when I was a regular on the city buses. If the bus was relatively empty and someone got on who was scratching, coughing, dishevelled, and breathing a toxic mixture of alcohol and cigarettes, that person would inevitably choose to sit beside me. He or she would also quickly become a candidate for jettisoning at the first signs of slumber.

There's always someone on the bus! There was an elderly man sitting with his travelling companion and they had apparently lost their luggage. Obviously, that would put anyone in a foul mood. In fact, his mood was so foul that they refused to move when the daily rotation took place. In spite of the cajoling and outright demands of their fellow passengers and guide, they would not budge. So it was as if that row of seats did not exist and everyone prayed that they would not land next to the disgruntled couple in the daily lottery. I like to think that holidays are a time for relaxing and having a good time, but some are just not capable of doing that, it seems. We found that out again on a cruise, but that story is for later.

Of course, as in any community, some bus travellers can be mean. Okay, maybe we can all be a little mean as we become more travel weary! The last person to board the bus is often

I GUESS WE MISSED THE BOAT

met by a chorus of hoots and hollers, especially if they are late. One day, bus traveller Bob, who was travelling by himself, was so wrapped up in whatever it was he was looking at that the bus started to pull away without him. By this time, people had become familiar with Bob and began yelling, "Where's Bob?" From then on the running gag was if Bob was onboard, everyone was onboard.

Scotland is a beautiful country, but there was one thing that bothered me. Don't get me wrong. I love the Scottish people, the landscape, the food, the beer. I am not so keen on the reputed weather, but we were lucky during the time we were there. The weather was pretty good. In fact, I think we probably used up all the good days Scotland had been allotted for that year.

I even found out during our visit that I am of Scottish descent, so I should love the place! It was a shock. I always thought I was descended from the Irish until we visited Braemar Castle in Scotland, home of the Clan Farquharson. We were sauntering through the hallowed halls when Evelyn (who is of Scottish descent) gleefully pointed out a family tree on the wall. There, prominently displayed, was the name "Finlay." What the heck!? For most of my life I had kind of enjoyed telling people I was Irish, but I guess I have to change my bonnie wee tune. Evelyn even bought a blanket in the colours of the Farquharson Tartan as a constant reminder of my heritage.

So, what could it be that bothers me about Scotland? It's not the people, the weather, the scenery . . . No, it's none of those. In fact, I love Scotland and will hopefully go back one day. But there's one thing that I'm not at all fond of in Scotland. It's those bagpipes!! I don't like bagpipes. I should rephrase that. I like them from a distance. But I like them even better when they are far enough away that I can't hear them. The sound they make often grates on my nerves. Comparing it to stepping on a cat's tail would be too easy. I'm not sure what to compare it to.

A few of us from the tour decided to go to a local pub one night for some refreshments and entertainment. We might have known that the entertainment could be bagpipes, but there are other traditional types of Scottish music, right?

We walked in, and a number of Scottish heads at the bar snapped around to see who the newcomers were. They murmured among themselves, and we were left standing as there wasn't an empty seat in the place, which must mean the entertainment is going to be good. I went into the bathroom and had just got settled at the urinal when in walked one of the locals. He was wearing a kilt and had red hair and a full red beard. He looked pretty normal, for a Scot, but he was carrying with him an instrument of torture. He was carrying his bagpipes and he was there to "tune" them. Imagine, if you will, being trapped in a concrete cell block of about ten feet by ten feet with no visible means of escape. That would be enough to drive anyone crazy. Then add to that the sound of someone "tuning" his bagpipes! It could be a way to force a confession from a terrorist, although I doubt it would meet the terms of the Geneva Convention, which establishes certain rights for the *humane* treatment of prisoners of war.

I am sure it sounded great to some. The gentleman must have known somehow that his bagpipes were in tune for he had a look of ecstasy on his face as he blew into the blow stick and pumped vigorously on the bag of his precious "musical" instrument. As the sound pounded through my head, I was somehow able to excuse myself and find the exit. As I burst out through the door into the main area of the bar, my travelling companions broke out in gales of laughter when they saw the look of horror on my face. The locals at the bar all looked bemused, wondering how some dumb tourist from across the pond could not be grateful for the private audition. As I sidled up to Jim, I could hear him say in a voice that sounded to my ringing ears as if it was coming from the other side of town, "Hey, Barry, do you know the definition of a *gentleman*?"

"NO, JIM, WHAT IS IT?"

"It's someone who knows how to play the bagpipes, but doesn't."

I couldn't agree more!

We visited Glasgow, Edinburgh, and northern Scotland. We saw the Loch Ness (but no monster) and we stopped at St.

Andrews. Although there was no time to play a round of golf, I was encouraged to see someone flub their shot off the first tee like anyone else. The heather was in bloom when we drove through the countryside so the moorlands were ablaze with the low-lying shrubs laden with purplish flowers. On the hills and in the valleys, we spotted herds of Highland Cows or "heeland coos" as they're known locally. This caused some excitement among the farmers. Highland cows are similar to Canadian cows by virtue of having four legs. But their coats are long and wavy, much of it hanging over the animal's face, giving them the appearance of not having a clue where they're going or, for that matter, where they've been. The ones we saw had long horns and their coats were a reddish brown colour. They are indeed beautiful animals, but in spite of their gentle appearance with their hair hanging in their eyes, I doubt very much if you would want to mess with one.

One of the highlights, at least for some, was a visit to Crathie Kirk, which is a small church in Scotland and the place of worship for the Royals when they are staying at Balmoral. It's built of local granite with a pine roof. We were supposed to see Balmoral, but the Queen has a habit of getting in our way as we will discuss later on in the conversation. Balmoral is a wee piece of Scottish land (about forty-nine thousand acres) and is one of the royal residences. Yes, we were supposed to visit Balmoral, but the Queen and Duke were staying there so we didn't get to see it.

I guess the next best thing to seeing Balmoral was our visit to Crathie Kirk so we got to see a small old church that looks a lot like other small old churches in the UK. As we were about to leave, we were told that we would be sticking around just a little bit longer. We were also told that the Queen would be opening a small fair just down the road. We did hang around and a small motorcade of three cars drove by. There was the Queen herself looking a bit startled by the small crowd of commoners milling around her church. After a few seconds, she recovered her royal self and the hand shot up to give us the royal wave. It was pretty exciting to see Her Majesty just a few feet away.

One of the "get acquainted" parties on this tour featured Scottish entertainment, a few drinks, and . . . haggis. There were a few groans around the room at the reminder of this delicacy. It's a pudding containing tidbits from the heart, liver, and lungs of a sheep and seasoned with onion, oatmeal, suet, spices, and salt, mixed with flavoured water. As if the thought of the heart, lungs, and liver wasn't bad enough, suet is mutton fat, generally taken from *around* the liver. To top it off, the whole tasty mix is usually wrapped in the animal's stomach, although sausage may also be used. I thought it wasn't half bad. That could mean one of three things: the cooks might have taken it easy on the tourists and used other ingredients, or they had plied us with enough drink that we couldn't have cared less, or it really *wasn't* that bad. Some of our party would disagree with the latter hypothesis.

Just as we are about to leave this subject of Scotland, the Royal Mile comes up. The Royal Mile leads up to the Edinburgh Castle, which stands majestically at the top. It absolutely controls the skyline of Edinburgh. It is believed people actually lived there as long ago as the ninth century. And the route up to it is the equivalent of a Scottish mile. Now there's a piece of trivia for you. Did you know that a Scottish mile is longer than our mile and an Irish mile is even longer? A mile isn't a mile nor is it a mile, apparently. Evelyn chimes in at this point to remind us that she had told us travel was a learning experience.

More important, the Royal Mile is a series of shops, outdoor vendors, and pubs guaranteed to make the most hardened tourist salivate. It was there that Ed the Negotiator added one more chapter to his legend. He made a vendor cry on the Royal Mile in Edinburgh! Well, that might be a slight exaggeration, but you know how the Scots like their money. Ed managed to pry some Celtic rings out of the vendor's grasp at a fraction of the asking price. I'm sure the vendor was left asking, "What just happened?" It's probably just as well that he didn't know Ed is of English heritage.

I had a feeling we would go back to Scotland one day, and it came sooner than I expected. It wasn't long before we were once again in the land of haggis, castles, bagpipes (groan), and the most frugal people on the planet. "Ed, are you *sure* you're not Scottish?"

8

JIM RECOUNTS A STORY he heard about a fine Scottish lad who was in a pub on Saturday night, as we understand most are. "He'd had a few drinks when he noticed two large women by the bar. They both had strong accents so he asked, "Hey, are you two ladies from Scotland?" One of them growled back, "It's WALES, you Scottish lout." So, the gentleman immediately apologized and said, "Sorry . . . Are you two whales from Scotland?"

Unwittingly, Jim gave us a nice segue into our next trip. The eight of us were off to Scotland again as part of a United Kingdom and Ireland tour. As Tina Turner sings in "Proud Mary," "We never ever do nothing nice and easy; we always do it nice and rough." It was kind of like that on our UK bus tour. There are slow bus tours that are known as leisurely paced, there are others that are medium paced, and then there are some that take place at a fast pace. We opted for warp speed. It became known as the "drive-by shooting" tour as we raced around the UK snapping photos from our bus that turned out to be blurry trees or the sides of trucks as they whizzed by.

We saw England, Scotland, Ireland, and Wales in eight days. I am not sure we really "saw" them, but we got a taste of each one and it was enough to want to go back. As usual, there were some highlights and stories that came out of the tour that shall never be forgotten.

We had some time in London to have a look around before the tour started so we decided the best use of our time would be to take a double-decker bus with on-off privileges. It was great. We stopped near Buckingham Palace and wandered around. We saw London Bridge twice as we made our way around. We took pictures of all the major sights in London, including the London

Bridge, the changing of the guard, Buckingham Palace, No. 10 Downing Street, and more.

We disembarked at one point to take a boat cruise down the Thames. That's when the trouble started. Oh, it wasn't the boat ride. It was awe inspiring as we got to see many of the sights of London we wouldn't have otherwise seen and we saw the London Bridge again. No, it was when we were going to get back on the bus. We all found that we were more than a little disoriented. Do we catch the bus on the north side of the street or the south side? Good question!! There were arguments for both. As in any democracy, everyone tried to absolve themselves of any responsibility and accountability by saying, "Well, if YOU think it's the north, we'll take that route," which was offset by, "Well, if YOU think it's the south, we'll take that route." That way, just like in any parliamentary system, we all had someone to blame when we followed the wrong choice.

This dance of democracy had lasted for a few minutes when we decided we couldn't just stand there. And just like any democracy, our decision was helped along by something fortuitous that took the choice completely out of our hands. A bus appeared in the distance on the opposite side of the road and the sisters agreed that we should all run to catch it. Of course, it was the wrong bus. But we did get to see London Bridge again from four different angles. If London Bridge ever does fall down, we collectively have more photos of it than anyone could possibly absorb and we would be happy to pass them out to anyone who might have missed the bridge.

They were the last clear pictures we took. We raced off on our sprint via bus the next day. It started out slowly enough. We visited Shakespeare's birthplace. I never was a big fan of Bill's literary works, but it was interesting to see where he was born. Then it was off to Anne Hathaway's cottage. Ron the Cowboy asked on the way if Anne Hathaway hadn't starred in some Western movie. Jim looked at him incredulously. "You mean *Brokeback Mountain*? *You* actually *watched* that?" Ron caught himself, and said, "Uh, no, it must have been something else." Finally, to make us all a little less uncomfortable, Ed pointed out that it wasn't THAT Anne Hathaway whose house we were going to see! This one wasn't a movie star to anyone's knowledge. I'm quite certain there were people on the bus hoping to catch a glimpse of the Hollywood star. Maybe some of them even signed on to this tour thinking that they might be able to get an autograph. Unfortunately, for them and, well, for all of us really, this one was Shakespeare's wife.

We think buildings are old at one hundred years in Canada. Shakespeare married Hathaway in 1582 so the cottage is well over four hundred years old. Does anyone think our modern-day structures will still be around four hundred years down the road? By the way, Hathaway was pregnant at the time of the marriage, leaving some to believe that it was a shotgun wedding. Just sayin'.

We raced through the English countryside and up to Scotland, dashed through Glasgow, and caught our breath for a few minutes in Edinburgh. I am fairly certain I saw hiking trails in northern England but I almost needed a chiropractic treatment as my head snapped around to see them pass by. It wasn't Fifty Shades of Grey but it was certainly the Forty Shades of Green that Johnny Cash sang about through the English, Scottish, and Irish countryside. It was made even more brilliant as the many shades of green were thrown into a blender with blues and yellows and came out in a continuous splash of colour as we charged on in our mighty Mercedes speed wagon.

We managed to arrive in Dublin at the same time as the Queen. Here she is again, getting in our way! It was the first time that the Queen had visited Ireland in over one hundred years, and there was excitement everywhere among the Irish. She managed to disrupt our tour to some extent. There were policemen every ten feet on the streets. Because of the intense security, we were required to go along unplanned routes, to leave earlier than expected, and to entirely miss some things we were supposed to see.

Ron the Cowboy reminds us that we were supposed to visit the Irish national stud farm where we could see world class stallions but were rerouted to a silver factory because the Queen was going to the farm and she seemed to have some sort of priority. Linda remarks how disappointed Ron was that the visit to the stud farm was cancelled. I can just imagine. This is a man who grew up around horses. I've seen him talking quietly to them and the horses listening to him in return. If they disobey, he can discipline them so they clearly feel that they have done something they weren't supposed to do. When they see him coming, they vie for his attention.

While he's no longer the wild team penning rider, there's still a bit of the cowboy in him and he takes children and adults on gentle sleigh and carriage rides and trail rides in the country. The horses respond with tremendous respect and affection. I think everyone felt disappointed when he didn't get to see one of the attractions he was most looking forward to. The Newbridge Silverware Company in Kildare, Ireland, was substituted for the stud farm and, while it was pretty impressive, it didn't quite measure up for Ron. I bought a nice pen, and we were off and running again.

Even though we were making a valiant attempt to break the world land speed record in our bus, the Prime Minister of the United Kingdom, David Cameron, and his entourage blasted by us like we were standing still in black vehicles with darkened windows. The telltale sign that it was David Cameron, or someone purporting to be David Cameron, was the flags on the vehicles.

One of the attractions in Dublin is a statue of Molly Malone. Molly was a fictional character, but the song about her is Ireland's unofficial anthem. The statue depicts a young lady who is very well endowed indeed, pushing a cart. She is so well endowed, in fact, that her "endowments" appear to be falling out of her dress. According to our guide, the statue is known locally as the "Tart with the Cart."

The Irish have a great sense of humour and are a joy to be around. There is a monument that stands in close proximity to the Liffey River, known as the Spire of Dublin. However, since the locals seem to make fun of everything and since the spire has a phallic appearance, they just can't help themselves.

Among other things, the monument is known locally as the Stiffey by the Liffey!

I can't make this stuff up!

I imagine they have learned to find humour where they can after years of strife. We found the Irish to be among the friendliest and nicest people we have run into on the planet.

We were introduced to castle after castle, which made Evelyn very happy although most of us stayed in the bus for the last one. We saw some of the most expensive crystal in the world at the Waterford factory. Then we headed for South Wales. It is a picturesque ferry crossing to Wales, and the boat was full of sports fans in brightly coloured jerseys carrying brightly coloured flags and wearing brightly coloured scarves. They were rather large, they were rugby fans, it was eleven a.m., and some had been celebrating for some time. Some were sound asleep in various places on the ferry. I worked up the courage to ask what the excitement was about and got a look for my efforts as if I had just arrived from Mars. I tried to explain my obvious lack of grey matter:

"I'm from Canada. I'm a hockey fan."

"Oh, okay, mate! It's the European championships."

"So who am I hoping for?"

"The Irish, of course."

"Of course!"

I have no idea who won. Nor do I really care. I do know there were eighty-five thousand people at the game and it was party time in Cardiff. We didn't get to participate. We were on the warp speed tour and it was time to move on.

Speaking of old, the next stop was Bath where the temple was constructed around 70 AD! One can't help but stare in awe at the construction and intricate designs created so long ago by people with rudimentary tools. With modern-day tools that are specialized for every conceivable task, have we really progressed? It's a worthwhile question when you consider our modern-day architecture that will not withstand the ravages of time.

We were allowed to tour the baths but we weren't allowed to actually go into the water. I don't think that's a bad thing as it appeared to be a little murky. There were still some of the original

Romans hanging around. At least I assume they were originals as they were dressed in period outfits. I have to admit they have aged rather well and so has their clothing. Some of them must be over two thousand years old by now! I can only assume that they have special privileges at that age and are allowed to enter the water after the tourists have gone home. Despite its murky appearance, that water must have amazing rejuvenating powers!

The final pit stop just before we received the checkered flag for finishing first in our race across the UK and Ireland occurred at Stonehenge. What a magnificent structure it is, too. It is a circular series of stones standing upright with cross members across the top. This structure is even older than the Roman baths, dating back as far as 3000 BC. Theories abound as to why it's there and how it was constructed. There is a theory that some of the stones were dragged some 150 miles to be placed on the structure. Unfortunately, we are unable to ask the Romans back at Bath because they were born one thousand years too late! And even if they were old enough, when you consider how our memories are as we reach into our sixties and seventies, can you imagine what they must be like when you reach the age of two thousand?? They can probably barely remember to go to work in the morning!

Carbon dating is helping to unravel some of the secrets of Stonehenge, but we may never know exactly why some things are the way they are. But isn't that all right? Isn't it nice that there are some unanswered questions so that we can ask ourselves why and ponder the meaning of things? If I was given the opportunity to learn how a magician does a trick, I would decline with thanks. For me, some things are better unknown. I would rather listen to theories about Stonehenge than be certain of the real answers so that I can continue to marvel and gaze in awe.

Even though we all had a fine collection of blurry pictures to add to our albums at the end of the warp speed tour, perhaps the most interesting comment about seeing so many sights in a short period comes from a friend. She was disappointed after visiting London that she had not had the opportunity to see Big Ben. It's obviously one of the landmarks of the city and pretty hard to miss. She lamented to her husband all the way home that it was so unfortunate that she had not seen Big Ben.

She got home and, after uploading her pictures from her digital camera to her computer, she started to go through them. One of the photos gave her pause. As she stared at it, she could see herself with a big satisfied smile on her face and Big Ben looming over her shoulder in the background.

I look at pictures and even if they are as clear as possible, I often forget where they were taken or what the significance was at the time. I guess the answer is to create an album with a description for each photo before the location is forever lost in our memory banks.

The tour bus option is a great way to travel. There is no need for someone to miss the sights because they are spending too much time watching the road. The tourists really do forge friendships in the time they are together, although often promises to keep in touch are forgotten as the reality of home sets in. The guides are fully versed in the area and extremely friendly and willing to answer questions. They are also quite understanding of the mood in the bus so when everyone's attention span is failing, they put on some soft music and just let the passengers reflect on what they've seen or have a nap if they wish.

As for England, Scotland, Ireland, and Wales, the countryside is beautiful and the people are incredibly friendly. There is something to be learned from the Irish with their self-deprecating sense of humour. They laugh at everything, in spite of the strife that has gone on there for years. There will be more bus tours and I hope we get to go back to that part of the world. I recommend opting for anything below the warp speed tour.

Just before we came into the hotel from lunch to start this reflective discussion, Jim had noticed a mint condition 1957 Chevrolet on the street. A car of that vintage and in that kind of shape can bring most men to their knees. It's something we males have ingrained in us. We all appreciate a good shape. The men in this group love vehicles and we all like to think the ladies appreciate a nice vehicle, too. It's only natural that the conversation switches to travel by automobile.

9

LINDA RE-ENTERS the room trailing the slight odour of eau du smoke. "Are you talking about cars again, Jim? I could have stayed outside longer, enjoying the fresh air! Bor-r-r-i-n-g!" This just might have been a preemptive strike to deter any comments about smoke. The best defence is a good offence and all that. In spite of the laughter from the other ladies, we soldier on in the direction of travel by automobile.

Evelyn and I grew up in central Canada along with the rest of the group in the room, but we were the only ones who moved away for career reasons. We moved to eastern Canada and spent a lot of time driving for two and a half days to visit our parents, siblings, and other assorted relatives back home. We even made the trek once with our two sons in our 1985 two-door Thunderbird.

I mention that my first vehicle was not actually a car. My first motorized mode of transportation was a two-stroke 125 cc BSA motorcycle that was manufactured in the fifties. I think it gave my mother nightmares when I bought it. In fact, I'm not even sure I got permission. I had it for a summer, but dumping it on a gravel road resulted in the end of its brief life with me. That isn't to say I wouldn't ride a motorcycle again. There's something about riding along on a hot day with the wind in your hair. The bugs in the teeth can be a little distracting but can be ignored. I just decided that I wanted something with four wheels. I saved my money and bought a 1957 Chevrolet. It was the same model as the beauty we had seen outside but mine wasn't in quite the same shape. I bought mine for $125 and I have to admit it came with a few warts.

It didn't have the fancy accoutrements of some of the vehicles my brothers-in-law owned in their early years. There were no fender skirts, whip aerials, or continental kits. Brenda says she remembers the name, continental kits, but can't remember what they are. Ron explains that they're often ornamental or may hold a spare tire on the back bumper.

But everyone in the room is old enough to remember the vacuum windshield wipers that slowed when the accelerator was pressed and that would come to a complete stop as the car sped up. They worked well as soon as the car reached cruising speed. They were a step up from the original crank wipers that required the driver to turn a lever to make the wipers work. But it always became a little uncomfortable when climbing a hill with the accelerator pressed to the floor in a crashing thunderstorm with the rain coming at the car sideways and no windshield wipers! It was always a relief to reach the top of the hill so the wipers would begin to work again.

My Chev had another little quirk that made it distinct from most of the rest. Well, maybe two quirks. I let the group in on its shortcomings. There were holes in the floorboards through which the ground was visible. Although that in itself was a little disconcerting, the real issue was travelling on the gravel roads that were prevalent in rural Manitoba. The interior of the vehicle was soon blown so full of dust that it was almost impossible to see. The good news was that I didn't need the windshield wipers when the roads were dusty. That would have been double jeopardy!

The second quirk manifested itself when the car was parked. It was never difficult to find the car, especially if it was parked on a hill. It leaked . . . water *and* oil. Like Hansel and Gretel leaving a trail of bread crumbs, there would always be a path of water and oil leading me to where it was parked. I got the feeling it always thought it had been kidnapped when I left it for any extended period of time and it would leave its distinguishing mark for me so I could find it. I always carried a quart of oil and a gallon of water to replenish the supply before moving on to our next destination.

That proud little vehicle with all its faults went down in a blaze of glory. I sold it to someone in the area who was older than me and I subsequently found out that it met its end in a demolition derby. I didn't witness the final battle; it would have been like watching a friend being fed to the lions, but I'm sure it fought the good fight to the bitter end.

There is a moment of silence in the room as we all think about that car. Fortunately, because of the toughness ingrained in us from growing up on the prairies, no one sheds a tear. Thoughts quickly turn to newer cars that we have owned. My 1985 Thunderbird was a beautiful car. Definitely, it was one of my favourites! Sleek, black, sunroof. It looked like it was going seventy miles an hour when it was standing still and it got admiring glances everywhere it went. But there was one drawback to my Thunderbird for a family of four.

Evelyn and I had the opportunity on many occasions to travel with our children, being the proud parents of two boys. They are normal, wonderful boys, and two of the greatest achievements my wife and I have accomplished. Travelling with children, of course, introduces a whole new dimension to the experience at the best of times. All of our companions had similar experiences to ours as we reminisce about travelling with our offspring. Most were smart enough not to go too far with kids in tow. However, since we wanted to make the annual two-and-a-half-day trek back to see the family, we loaded the kids up and away we went.

There wasn't much room for Trevor and Chris in the back seat of the two-door Thunderbird. To make it much worse, Trevor just had to take his guitar on the trip west and the only place for it was in the back seat. He was twelve at the time and his brother was eight years old. Needless to say, Chris insisted on his half of the seat, and there was no one or nothing that would be allowed to infringe on his space.

Trevor was very attached to that guitar. Later, when he was in high school, his picture appeared with his guitar in the couples section of the yearbook. After much discussion, we finally agreed that he could take his guitar, provided that we didn't hear any complaints. Evelyn threatened to leave the guitar on the side of the road if he complained. It was an idle threat but

I GUESS WE MISSED THE BOAT

we think he got the picture. He sat there for two and a half days going west and again coming back east with his guitar between his legs. We would stop at a restaurant, and I would leave the door open, waiting for Trevor to unravel his legs from the guitar so that he could come in and eat. We would watch him from the restaurant window until he was safely inside. The results of his perseverance and dedication are apparent today as he pursues his career as a professional musician. We ask ourselves what would have happened if he had not been allowed to take his guitar on that trip, and the answer is always the same. He would still be following his passion and doing what he loves.

We had had experiences travelling with the kids, or at least kid, before we moved. For some reason, before our second son was born, Evelyn and I decided to travel to Wyoming's Yellowstone National Park from our home in Manitoba with our elder son in tow. Trevor was eleven months old and had started running as soon as he could walk. We had very little money so the only way we could accomplish such a trip was by camping. Everything was lining up for an adventure. An eleven-month-old, a tent, no experience with camping, and, for my mother, a sense of impending doom. As we were throwing the tent and baby seat in the car, she stood wringing her hands. "This will lead to divorce," she proclaimed in her best doomsayer voice with a tear in her eye. "Don't be silly," we naively shouted back as we headed down the driveway with the car laden with all the camping and baby equipment we could possibly need.

Except for metal tent pegs!

Oh, we had tent pegs. But they were plastic! And upon arriving at the camping site in Minot, North Dakota, which we had strategically pre-booked, we discovered the sites were solid bedrock. Good thing I had a hammer! I pounded on those pegs until they bent but I got them in . . . to a degree. I would find out later it was not quite far enough but I was satisfied for the time being. The next order of business was to pump up the air mattresses. How hard can this be? I had a hand pump and I started pumping. About five minutes after I began, a truck with a camper trailer pulled up in the next campsite. He hopped out, waved, cranked the handle on the camper, and plugged it into the electrical outlet, walked to the fridge, popped open a beer, sat on his lawn chair, and watched.

I was still pumping and getting redder, partly from the exertion but more from the ignominy, feeling his bemused gaze on my back as he sipped on his nice cool beer. Every time I looked up, he would tip his hat, toast me with the beer, give me a wry smile, and take another sip. Finally, he drifted over with an electric pump in hand and asked if I thought this might help. "Yes, thank you," I growled as I took it from his hands and finished pumping up the mattresses.

He invited me over when I was finished, and as we sat by his camper and gazed across at our now completed campsite, I learned his name was Bob. He was seventy-five years old and worked at Home Depot in Baton Rouge, Louisiana. I asked how he came to be working at the age of seventy-five. He said, "Well, I retired fifteen years ago and I found I just couldn't sit still. I knew that somthin' needed to be done. Finally, one day, I said to my wife, 'Honny, I love you more than a pig loves its slop but I've got to do somethin' to get outta the house!' 'I went and sat outside the building site of a new Home Depot that was under construction until someone who looked like management came out.' He said, 'Can I help you?' I said, 'Yessir, you can give me a job.' He said, 'What can you do?' I said, 'I don't know.' He said, 'Can you do plumbing?' I said, 'Yessir!' and I have been in the plumbing department ever since." Bob was a very cool individual, and as the sun went down we shared a beer (one of his because mine were warm).

I went back to our campsite, and as Evelyn and I sat by the fire, the breeze was wafting softly through the trees causing the leaves to rustle slightly. The moon could be seen drifting in and out of the clouds. So this is why people camp! But that night that calm breeze that had been cooling the air and causing the trees to moan softly rose up off its bed, started spinning its head 360 degrees and shouting obscenities at everyone in the campsite as it turned into a raging gale force wind! The sides of the tent wavered, first a little, then a lot as the wind got stronger.

I GUESS WE MISSED THE BOAT

Our tent pegs held mightily for a few minutes, but the gale was just too much for the sad, bent little yellow plastic pegs that were keeping us separated from the elements. The elements eventually won and the side of the tent came in on our faces. Up out of the warm sleeping bag and out into the wet cold I went to try to salvage my pride and, oh yes, the tent. A little more hammering in the quiet of the night and we were back in business, at least until morning.

Trevor slept soundly through the whole ordeal, but I think he was probably the only one in the immediate area as I was once again outside hammering feverishly on the tent pegs. In fact, I'm quite sure if anyone had seen my silhouette with hammer in hand against the soft light of the flashlight illuminating the inside of the tent, the local SWAT team would have converged on Lot 127 to subdue the maniac before further damage was done.

This seemed like all part of the adventure to us, as we continued on our way the next morning, headed for Wyoming. Beautiful open spaces passed us by as we cruised along the highway, the sun shining down upon us from the country of the big sky. Mother Nature had given us a beautiful day, our son was happy in the back seat, the music was on, we had our windows down and the wind was blowing our hair, and we were revelling in the fact that Mom was wrong. This could well be the best vacation ever, plastic tent pegs and wind notwithstanding. We did notice a darkening on the horizon as we sped along.

We had driven through some of the most beautiful country imaginable. The Rocky Mountains were in the distance; the land was mostly flat but was slowly swelling into rolling foothills. The sun was glistening off the golden crops, creating the potential for a magnificent watercolour painting. Maybe I shouldn't have mentioned water. Having grown up on the prairies, I know that approaching storms in the west sharpen the senses. You can see them coming. You can smell it in the air. You can hear the distant thunder.

There was a layer of moisture hovering over the land in the distance, like the sheet on a bed; only this one was perpendicular to the ground. We could see the streaks in the white and grey sheet that was advancing toward us. It was interspersed with jagged lightning strikes that lit up the ever-darkening sky. Up went the windows as it arrived. A deluge of biblical proportions descended upon us . . . for a few minutes. The windshield wipers worked valiantly to keep the windows clear with minimal success. I was peering through the torrents of rain, trying to keep to the right of the centre line that was appearing and disappearing in front of our eyes.

But just as quickly as it arrived, it stopped. It was a deluge for sure but a short one and since we appeared to be in a rain-free zone once again, down went the windows so we could savour the electrical current that hung in the air and the sweet smell of newly wet grass. As we drifted alongside a park in quaint Miles City, Montana, the sky was still black around us, but beautiful sunshine beckoned to us from the horizon with its tendril-like fingers of light, urging us to keep coming . . . to push on. But it was a set-up.

The clouds that we thought had passed us by erupted and emitted a startling bright flash and a thunderous Cr-a-a-ac-k! A lightning bolt struck in the park a few hundred feet from my naked arm dangling out the window. My arm that had been a tanned golden brown colour only seconds before now appeared to be stark white to match my pale face as every hair on my arm and neck stood at attention. The drill sergeant in the form of the lightning had spoken, and the soldiers represented by the hairs on my arm were definitely listening. I slowly drew my arm into the car, thinking that I was very happy it was still attached and would be able to hang out the window another day. In the meantime, up went the windows for the last time that day.

Still, this was an adventure, right? What else could happen? Trevor was in great humour and enjoying the trip, making it easier on all of us. We set up the tent at our campsite in Yellowstone Park, much quicker this time as we had picked up metal pegs and an electric pump and I was really starting to get the hang of this camping thing. Unfortunately, there are rattlesnakes in the area, so my job was to check the tent before anyone entered to ensure that they hadn't chosen to invade our space. I have an aversion to snakes, but not as big as Evelyn's, so the task fell to me. None arrived, fortunately, but we quickly learned something. We had to watch our son every second from morning to night!

The one thing Trevor could do really well at this age was run, and he did! He was running here and running there. And our campsite was located next to a creek. We didn't want him to disappear or fall into the creek or any of the other dire things that can happen to an eleven-month-old so we got up at dawn, did the tourist thing, and reappeared at dusk, hoping that he would sleep. It became a ritual as we would return to the tent at dusk, exhausted from the daily task of trying to keep him occupied and under control. I would stand outside the tent, listening for rattles coming from the inside and, hearing none, I would gingerly enter the tent, stick in hand, praying that I would not encounter anything that slithered. Then we would put our son to bed. By the time I got the fire going each night, we were both so exhausted from the daily footrace that we would spend very little time actually sitting beside it. We were just too tired.

I assure everyone that Old Faithful is beautiful and worked like clockwork as it's supposed to. The scenery in America's oldest national park is magnificent with its bubbling geysers, mountains, lakes, and abundant wildlife. We got to know every inch of that park during the time we were there. It is truly one of the gems of the United States.

We survived that trip and it is etched in the memory banks as a memorable one. As we approached the Manitoba border on our way home, we were pretty satisfied with ourselves that our immediate plans did not include a trip to the lawyer to begin divorce proceedings. Trevor was asleep in his car seat as we pulled up to Canada Customs to answer the usual litany of questions and be on our way. Admittedly, we all looked pretty scruffy from our ordeal, er, I mean, vacation. I hadn't shaved during the trip, and the car was laden with camping gear. The Customs officer smiled a sinister smile and asked us to go to

Secondary. We dutifully did that knowing full well that the officer would see an eleven-month-old in the car seat and send us on our way.

What he did instead was remove everything from the back seat and put it on the ground. Our eleven-month-old had to be awakened and removed from the car along with his seat. Then everything from the trunk came out and was perfunctorily placed on the ground. Once everything had been removed, including the spare tire, he said we could go. He meant we could go as soon as *we* put everything back into the car!

My mom was standing expectantly in front of the house when we arrived and smiled when she saw there were three people in the car. No one got lost, no one was eaten by a bear, no one was bitten by a rattlesnake, and no one got divorced. And we had survived our last camping trip!

Travelling with the kids is a great experience and certainly creates family memories. Survival of a trip with kids makes us stronger. We all agree that, whether they realize it or not, it's also a great experience for the kids and one that they'll always remember. Our younger son, after staying in a bed and breakfast with us as a teenager in the beautiful Canadian province of Prince Edward Island, couldn't fathom why we would want to leave the colour television, pool, and all the comforts of home behind. Chris is now doing the same with his kids.

There was one more "travelling with the kids" story that I wanted to share with the group. Before launching into the story, I mentioned it involved mirrors in the bedroom. I could see eyebrows raise and sense that ears perked up. Ron even looked up from his Western novel! Here goes . . .

10

WE HAD TAKEN a weekend trip to Columbus, Ohio, for a conference. We loaded the kids into the car and off we went. The conference went well. We even got to ride in the elevator with some of the players for the NFL's Los Angeles Rams. They were there for an exhibition game and were staying in the same hotel as us. They were instantly recognizable because they were the only ones in the hotel with no necks. There were just these giant heads above shirts and pants that covered enormous bodies. I would have checked the weight restrictions on the sign in the elevator to see if we might be over the limit, but my view was blocked on all sides. After you, sir!

The conference ended and we turned the car toward home. Somehow, I became as sick as I had ever been to that point in my life. I couldn't drive. I couldn't hold anything down. I was miserable. We decided to find a hotel in Buffalo where I could curl up and die in peace. But there was nothing available due to some Monster Truck rally or Tractor Pull or something so back into the car we all went to continue driving.

The sun was setting, and Evelyn was driving down a dark, deserted road with trees on either side. We came across a motel that was barely visible with very few cars in the lot. One bulb lit the entrance to the motel, and the screen door squealed on its rusty hinges as we pushed it open and entered the darkened lobby. No one appeared at first as we huddled in the small space, wondering if the clerk was lying murdered beyond the walls that we were staring at. After Evelyn rang one of those little bells that make people magically appear, the clerk popped out like a jack-in-the-box, seemingly happy to see that other people still inhabited the planet.

One would think that all of this would be cause for concern, but since I felt like Norman Bates's preserved mother's corpse in *Psycho*, we thought we should give it a try. The office clerk gleefully told us that he had rooms available. He poked me in the ribs, which nearly started another round of vomiting, and told us that it was a suite so the boys would be sleeping in a different enclosed part of the room. We asked if we could see the room, and he said, "Of course!" and winked at me. Off they went to look, and I dragged my tired and aching body after them, hoping that I could lie down very soon and join Norman Bates's mom in the pickle jar. I felt a bit like Quasimodo dragging one leg behind me as we dodged the vines and cracks in the badly worn sidewalk along the side of the motel. We got to the room, and just like our friend said, there was a separate bedroom. "You're going to like this," said our exuberant clerk as he obliviously elicited another round of convulsions with a second poke in the ribs. Actually, I don't know if it was the shot to the ribs or the wink that almost made me throw up.

I know what the group is thinking as I make my way through this story. "Get to the mirrors, will ya!" Be patient, in-laws! Be patient!

Okay, here it comes. We went into the bedroom, and the bed was *surrounded by mirrored walls*. Great! We would be able to see my ghastly face with its sunken eyes and complexion of Casper the Friendly Ghost staring back at us as if we were sitting in an IMAX theatre! We took the room, and I slept the sleep of the dead without giving a second thought as to what may have transpired on the bedclothes an hour before we got there. Meanwhile, the rest of the family spent the night taking down cobwebs and removing spiders and fish flies from the room before the boys would even consider getting into bed. Evelyn decided if she turned off the light, the boys wouldn't be able to see any of the insects that remained. She sat guard duty for a while to ensure that our offspring didn't disappear in the clutches of some winged creature during the night.

I felt much better the next day. We fought our way through the grieving families of the fish flies that had met an untimely death in the battle of the night before. The survivors had taken

I GUESS WE MISSED THE BOAT

refuge on the outside of the door since the light that was attracting them to the inside was extinguished some time before dawn. Then we all piled into the car to complete our journey.

I had no idea why everyone else was in such a bad mood as we drove home!

I think the males in the group were disappointed that the mirror story wasn't a little more exciting and the females were clearly relieved. We continued with the stories related to travel by automobile . . . and on conveyances with four legs.

11

"IT MUST BE FIVE O'CLOCK somewhere! Time for a nice cold beer," says Ron. He loves his Budweiser and seems to be able to find it nearly every place we have gone in the world, although he did manage to choke down a Guinness in Scotland. He looks every bit the cowboy with his slim appearance and weathered, craggy face adorned with its large bushy mustache. That mustache has appeared in many forms, including my favourite, the Fu Manchu, but today it is a full, slightly greying masterpiece, just drifting over the top lip. He is sporting blue jeans and looks over the top of his reading glasses to make his announcement while turning another page in his Western novel.

Everyone agrees with his analysis of the situation, and it sounds like a few people are trying to discreetly attract each other's attention as the caps are slipped off the bottles, filling the air with that familiar, refreshing sound: P-s-s-s-s-t! Nothing goes better with beer than peanuts, and as Ron pries himself away from his novel and gets some from the fridge, he drops them on the floor. Jim, the Jokemaster, contributes, "Ron, it sounds like your nuts fell off."

Before we continue with the travel-by-automobile stories, there is one more form of conveyance we haven't touched on and that's the live variety. Ron is the perfect example. He talks about his horseback riding and team penning events in particular. He has an amazing talent with training horses and always has had since I've known him. As an example, team penning is a competition involving culling three identified cattle from a herd of thirty and directing them into a pen at the other end of the arena in a specific period of time, like a minute or a minute and a half. Who does that!? Well, Ron has until recently.

I have my own thoughts about horses and they're not

I GUESS WE MISSED THE BOAT

particularly pleasant. I grew up around large workhorses and don't have much experience riding. I was talked into trail riding once and, while I would have been quite happy on a motorcycle, riding something that big that was alive and not particularly happy about being taken out of its nice comfortable stall in the barn was not exactly where I wanted to be. I asked the trail ride leader to pick a nice quiet one and, when I was finally seated on the beast, I was told that I should be careful as the horse I was on liked to try to rid itself of its rider. It was a quiet horse all right; quietly plotting how it could dump me somewhere so it could go back to chomping on some nice, tasty, freshly mown hay.

So it brushed against fence posts and trees, trying its best to get rid of me, but I was equally determined not to be embarrassed by landing in a heap at its feet and giving it the satisfaction it was looking for. I could just see it snorting with its teeth bared and its big floppy lips quivering in a triumphant horse laugh.

I managed to stay on and complete the trail ride, muttering under my breath the entire time that this would be the last. But the horse did get the last laugh. The final indignation came when it sensed the barn and picked up its pace toward it. I was hanging on for dear life, feeling as if my body was straight out, parallel to its back, as it geared up through a trot to a full gallop. In actual fact, I was still seated as steed and terrified rider careened through the open door. At the last second, I was able to duck and avoid being knocked backwards off the horse. By this time, the horse didn't care as it was home and dreams of hay became reality.

No more horses for me, thanks, but I admire Ron for his ability to deal with those monsters. No, I much prefer my trail rides to be on lifeless, motorized vehicles and I prefer my travelling companions to have no more than two legs.

However, travelling with two-legged friends offers its own challenges along with the rewards. All I can say is they had better be very good friends or they won't be friends for long. We have undertaken the challenge on a few occasions. I reminded the group of our good friends, Don and Janet, with two daughters about the same age as our two boys, who went skiing with us in Vermont. They are divorced now so maybe Mom was right after all!

Don, Janet, Evelyn and I, and all the kids ventured by car to Florida one year to visit Disney World. Northerners like us who escape the cold are known as snowbirds in Florida, and Floridians have a deep appreciation for their northern neighbours. A bumper sticker we spotted while in Florida was evidence of that. It said, "If they are snowbirds, why can't we shoot them?" We were relieved to find that sentiment was not a common one.

It was a great trip for most of us. Unfortunately for Evelyn, the seagulls decided to use her as their personal bathroom. Everywhere we went, the seagulls would move into formation and come screaming in on strafing runs, raining their bombs down upon her unmercifully. Now Evelyn likes to take enough clothes for all weathers and every eventuality when we travel. Her suitcases and changes of clothing are legendary. She eventually worked her way through all of it thanks to the incredible

I GUESS WE MISSED THE BOAT

timing and accuracy of the seagulls. As well, only our youngest son would walk with her and the seagulls would inevitably miss him and hit Evelyn. It was pretty funny for those of us who weren't the victims, but we wondered why they were picking on her. Evelyn laughs about it to this day but she does suffer a little from post-traumatic stress disorder, having been shot at on the beaches of Florida.

Of course, any time you drive anywhere, it's great to have your own vehicle at your destination, but you will need a parking space. It's a "nice-to-have" item on your travels but it can also present challenges that have to be overcome. We learned that in New Jersey.

The previous Easter Sunday, Evelyn and I had driven to New York for the first time ever, so rather than driving in downtown New York, we decided to park the car in a multi-level parking garage in New Jersey and take the train to Grand Central Station. It was a great plan! We returned to our motel in New Jersey on the second last train from Manhattan, having just been in Times Square. It had been a great day in an amazing city. It was one o'clock in the morning and the parking garage where we had left the car seemed deserted. We took the elevator to the third floor of the concrete maze to retrieve the car.

I inserted my ticket into the machine to pay for our parking, and it was rejected. I tried it again. Rejected! I tried two other machines with the same result. Nothing! My mind was racing. How're we going to get out of this parking garage if we don't have a paid ticket to raise the barricade? I had visions of blasting through the barricade with a knife-wielding New Jersey gang hot on our tail.

There is a button on the machines to call the parking attendant. Tried that, no answer. In fact, I pressed the buttons on all three ticket machines and I could hear them all ringing at the attendant's booth two floors beneath us. Now my mind was really starting to race. This is New Jersey, after all. Feeling vulnerable? You betcha!

There was a police call box on the wall, which was comforting, but we decided to walk down to the first floor to see if we could find someone. I went to the attendant's booth where there was a sign that read, "Back in Ten Minutes." Who knew how long the sign had been there? Could this get any worse? I went to another machine and tried the ticket, only to be rejected again. I hammered on the door of the booth in case he was sleeping in the back. No reaction. I pressed the call button just so I could have the satisfaction of hearing yet another phone ringing somewhere in the booth. At least it created a sound. The parking lot had been—dare I say it—quiet as a tomb to that point.

I pause for dramatic effect and notice that everyone is waiting patiently for me to finish my story. Finally, Carol can't take it. "So what happened?"

Well, about twenty minutes later someone came strolling down the ramp from the second floor. I tensed until I could see who it was. I had my keys in my hand with one key protruding between my index and middle fingers, ready to ward off an attack. I had seen that on a television show once.

It was the attendant who had been making his rounds. I explained the problem and he apologized and tried the ticket. Nothing. He tried a new ticket. He said, "It won't be more than $5." "Um, no it certainly won't," I said. The maximum at night was $2, and with the mood I was in, he was seriously in danger of being stuffed into the nearest garbage can. Then I realized I probably wouldn't be able to do that since the garbage can was likely already full of tourists who had been trapped in the garage on previous nights. I also realized that if I did that, we still wouldn't be able to get out!

"Okay," he said with a shrug. "The system is down." Really!!?? Who knew? After trying a series of new tickets, he finally got one to work and the barricade miraculously rose. There were a few other cars waiting in the parking lot for their unsuspecting passengers who would be equally aggravated by the experience they had awaiting them. I think the parking lot attendant's night was about to become his worst nightmare when the last train arrived. "Have a good night," I said, cackling as we made our great escape from that concrete booby hatch.

Driving has its challenges and benefits, for sure. Things have been simplified by the GPS, although many of the people in this room have argued with the voice coming from the dashboard. No more maps as we rely on the electronic genius to lead us to our destination. While it's rarely wrong, it has occasionally led us astray. It tried to lead us off the side of a bridge into the water in Nashville, Tennessee, and it managed to get us lost in Columbus, Ohio, more than once. I'm sure when we figure out the difference between the terms "keep right," "bear right," and "turn right" and apply them properly, we'll be fine and travel by auto will be much simpler.

But with all the benefits of the GPS, there's one thing that we should all be wary of as we follow its instructions. As we blindly obey with no real awareness of the route we're pursuing, it's clearly making us dumber. To offset this, Evelyn stubbornly still manages to sneak maps into our car from time to time.

As we close out the discussion of travelling by car, we realize that we've all had some pretty good times in Henry Ford's invention. I think we've all come to the conclusion that we would rather spend two and a half days driving than being stuck on an overcrowded airplane for four hours.

It's time for some plane talk.

12

EVERYONE GETS UP and stretches. We've been sitting here for a while now. With the coffee pot refreshed and bathroom breaks taken, Joke-a-Minute Jim takes the opportunity to tell us another story. He asks us if we know that the inventor of the Hokey Pokey died recently. No one knew. Jim says with a perfectly straight face, "It was very traumatic for the family, of course. When they tried to put him into the coffin, they put his left leg in and that's when the trouble began."

After I stop laughing, my mind continues to wander through the halls of my own travelling experiences. Most of my early airplane trips across Canada were uneventful. I'm sure most people can attest to the routine. You wait at the airport, go through Customs, ride the plane, get off the plane, and do everything in your power to try to unplug your ears. Did I say wait at the airport? Just like we're doing now, it's always about killing time.

One of the most interesting things to do when waiting is to mindlessly watch the luggage carousel go around and around with its assortment of black luggage that all pretty much looks the same. Finally, one that looks similar to the one you left with the baggage handlers a few hours ago, only a little more battered, exits the chute, crashes against the sides of the carousel, lands upside down with its wheels in the air like a turtle trying to right itself, and finally makes its way to its rightful owner.

I was experiencing yet another one of those mind-numbing routines in the airport in Winnipeg, Manitoba, when a bulging suitcase rocketed down the chute and came to an ignominious end with a thud against the edge of the carousel. I don't use the word "end" loosely as there was the sound of a tiny explosion and the case burst open and shot an unfortunate woman's delicates all over the carousel. I did the gentlemanly thing and averted my gaze so that I wouldn't see the collection of bras and panties that were now draped across the other black suitcases piling up against the yawning maw of the bag that was now lying open. It reminded me of a fish on land gasping for air. I didn't notice the red, pink, and black bikini panties or the low-cut matching bras or the sexy white negligee that was hanging half in and half out of the suitcase. I didn't notice that it was so sheer that you could see the contents of the suitcase through the thin diaphanous material. The thought did flash through my head that surely that material is one of the wonders of modern science and its developer has been aptly rewarded with the Nobel Prize by now.

No, I didn't see any of that. What I did see was the collection of males grinning and waiting to see who came and picked up the contents. I believe that the woman made the choice of discretion over valour as the only person that came forward was an airport attendant with a cardboard box. He scooped up the underwear and the broken suitcase and disappeared into the baggage claims area. I'm quite sure the embarrassed woman who had apparently melted into the crowd reappeared shortly afterwards at the claims desk.

Of course, one of the highlights of travelling is celebrity sighting. I assume it is much more rewarding in the celebrity sighting department in first class, but alas, that is not my lot in life. It's still possible to occasionally spot celebrities going through most of the same routines we do, albeit with a little more attention. Recently, Evelyn and I met Billy Ray Cyrus at the Nashville International Airport. Everyone's heard of Billy Ray. He sang "Achy Breaky Heart," one of those songs that no one admits to liking but everyone sings along and dances to.

As he passed through security ahead of us, we confirmed with the woman checking us in that it was indeed Billy Ray Cyrus. She said she couldn't understand what the fuss was about because she sees these people all the time. We did get a chance to talk to him briefly, and he is, without a doubt, one of the nicest celebrities that you could ever want to meet. As we continued on our way to our gate, a woman was walking in front of us talking on her cellular. She had met him as well and she seemed to be excitedly talking with a son or daughter. We couldn't help but hear her exclaim, "I just met Miley Cyrus's dad!" I guess celebrity is a fleeting thing! Or it could be simply a generation gap!

On a business trip to the east coast, my colleague and I were on the same plane as the rock band Platinum Blonde. I guess they hadn't quite made it to the big time yet because they were sitting in the cheap seats with the rest of us. With teenage sons at home, I was familiar with such things and I recognized them. I told my oblivious colleague who had never heard of them. Once I told him, he said he wanted to see them perform. Since we didn't have tickets it was going to be a challenge, but he said he would take care of it. That night, we made our way to the arena, and I naively assumed he had the tickets. My assumption seemed to be confirmed when we walked right past the box office.

We got to the ticket taker, and my colleague adopted a forlorn look and said, "My daughter is in there. She was forbidden from going to the concert and she is with someone I don't trust. Do you mind if my friend and I go in for a few minutes to find her?" I was aghast but silently tried to play along, hoping my face would not betray me for fear a pair of gigantic bouncers might appear to bounce us out onto the sidewalk. The sympathetic ticket taker who probably had daughters of her own told us to go ahead, and so off we went to look for his imaginary offspring. The elusive daughter would be in deep trouble . . . if she existed! We didn't spend much time looking, obviously, but we did find a couple of choice empty seats and enjoyed the show.

Coincidentally, I noticed recently that Platinum Blonde is making a comeback. Maybe celebrity isn't so fleeting after all! I guess if the same scenario unfolded today, it would have to be my colleague's granddaughter we were trying to find.

My celebrity sightings took a bizarre twist when I was travelling for work. Countless times as I was walking through the throngs at the airport, I would spot a distinguished-looking gentleman with long wavy white hair, deep creases in his broad face with its wide nose and deep-set eyes staring out from under bushy dark eyebrows. Sometimes his hair was braided with a band holding it in place. Once I saw him in a business suit, but more often he wore buckskin or other clothing distinguishing him as a proud Native Canadian.

He was Chief Dan George who was a real Indian chief of the Burrard Indian band in British Columbia, Canada. His claim to fame really began at age sixty when he started appearing on television and in the movies. He was most recognizable because of his appearances with Clint Eastwood in *The Outlaw Josey Wales* and with Dustin Hoffman in *Little Big Man*. He looked every bit the Indian chief, even when he wasn't in ceremonial dress, and he seemed to always appear at the airport like some ghostly apparition whenever I was there.

He was a stately man and because of his weathered and aged appearance, I always imagined he would be able to sit and dispense invaluable words of wisdom. I have often thought I should have introduced myself so that I could have benefited from some of those pearls. But I saw him so often, I began to think what I was seeing was some sort of spirit world emissary appearing to send me and my fellow passengers safely on our way. I imagined he might disappear in a puff of smoke if I approached him. Once I poked the next person in line and asked if he saw Chief Dan George. He said he did, but I wasn't convinced.

Chief Dan George died in 1981, but I often think of him sitting in the airport and, as I walk through, I'm sure he's still looking down and watching the passengers as they go about their travels. Most of all, I imagine he's smiling because he no longer has to put up with everything that drives most of us crazy about flying.

13

OF COURSE, to see some of the sights we've seen in airports, you have to fly, unless, of course, you just like to hang around airports to satisfy some weird fetish. Off we jetted to see the relatives in Manitoba. It was an uneventful trip . . . on the way there. It was routine as well on the way back until we heard the announcement. The captain came on and said that there was an electrical problem and that we would have to bypass Ottawa, our home and destination, and fly on to Montreal where they had more FIRE TRUCKS!

There are very few people who actually pay attention when the safety instructions are read, beyond keeping one eye open and thinking about their day, wondering if there is any possibility of getting peanuts on the flight. We all focus on pretty much anything but the instructions being presented right in front of us. Well, this was one of those announcements, until the words "fire trucks" came through loud and clear. It was mumble, mumble, mumble, FIRE TRUCKS. What!!?? Those two words will bring anyone out of their reverie! Would you please repeat the message? I promise I will listen this time!

Fortunately, it wasn't a long flight to Montreal so we didn't have much time to think. It appears that the problem was really a minor one or was resolved before we made our approach as we weren't told to put our heads between our legs in the correct position to kiss our asses goodbye. However, as we came in for a landing, there was a long row of flashing lights lining the runway, lighting up the fire trucks that were sitting there. The airplane landed without incident in spite of all the horrible things that went through our minds. We didn't have time to think until we were on another flight back to Ottawa, as we had to race from one end of the terminal to the other with two kids to get back on the plane the airline had graciously held for us.

Of course, that incident occurred when flying was simply a way of getting to a destination faster. It's much more than that now. Because there are weight restrictions, it all starts with the struggle to fit everything into a suitcase. No matter how large the luggage, there's never quite enough room. The traveller can fold, roll, and cajole their articles into the suitcase, but, inevitably, it comes down to cramming various pieces of clothing into every nook and cranny and using every muscle to force the suitcase closed. No one wants to repeat the experience of the exploding luggage described earlier.

Some people's suitcases are a little more packed than others. I will never forget the scolding I received from the airline attendant in Hawaii who told me with a growl that my (Evelyn's) suitcase was way too heavy, or riding on the bus in Scotland where there was a daily competition among the riders to determine whose suitcase was the heaviest. The ultimate goal is to pack it as full as possible while scraping in under the airline limit by a fraction of a pound and that, ladies and gentlemen, is an art.

This struggle of man against suitcase is followed closely by the epic journey to the airline counter for check-in. If the struggle with the suitcase has not fouled the intrepid traveller's mood completely, they will have had the wherewithal to check in online at home, saving copious amounts of time and embarrassment in a public place. If not, they are required to present themselves in front of the machine to acquire the mandatory boarding pass. There's usually an agent hovering nearby with a knowing smirk, waiting for the harried passenger to fail miserably in their attempt to make the machine work. Once the inevitable failure occurs, the agent swoops in to embarrass them within an inch of their life by demonstrating how easy it is to use the machine.

Once through that experience, it's time to meet the agents behind the desk. The service industry has its share of issues, undoubtedly, and it's amazing that some agents occasionally greet the passenger with a smile. In my experience, the best way to get service is to act pleasantly and to show a little empathy for the plight of the poor clerk. The clerks must get at least some enjoyment from the passengers as they struggle to get to the counter laden with their suitcases, books, puzzles, cameras, iPods, diaper bags, computers, etc., etc., but theirs is not an easy job. They must meet their fair share of ignorance in the form of angry, tired travellers. And sometimes the travellers are understandably impatient and upset.

Carol recounts the story of a cancelled flight and a lineup of unruly passengers trying to book on another airplane. It had been going on for hours, and the passengers were probably legitimately frustrated with the length of time it was taking to get on the next flight. The clerk had had enough and was on the verge of tears. One of the passengers arrived at the front of the line and started to show some empathy. "Are you fed up with your job? Feel like crying? Want to go home?" "Yes," said the clerk with a trembling voice, her misty eyes gratefully making contact with those of the passenger. "Good," said the passenger. "So do I! Now get me a ticket on the next available flight!!"

There is another sweat-inducing moment at the official weigh-in of the suitcases. My friend Wendy recently returned from a trip to Cuba that epitomized the anxiety that can occur at the official weigh-in. It's like a boxer who is on the borderline of his weight class. In order to meet the weight to be in a lower class, boxers have been known to strip down to their birthday suits. Well, it's kind of like that with the suitcases, only in reverse. It may come down to adding additional layers just so you don't have to carry them in your suitcase.

Wendy and her husband were on their way to Cuba and were standing near the front of a line of about forty people behind a well-dressed, slightly overweight woman whose suitcases were being weighed. The worst thing happened. The suitcases didn't meet their weight class at the official weigh-in. The woman had to open her suitcases in front of everyone and move some things around so that they weighed less. Wendy said, "She took out a pair of tiny shorts that maybe she shouldn't have been wearing anyway, along with some other things, and transferred them to her other suitcase and eventually she was allowed to move on." Wendy said to her husband, "Wouldn't that be embarrassing?" But then it occurred to her that she might have her own problem.

Anticipation is often the worst of all motivators as we all tend to build things up in our minds as we're waiting for a particularly uncomfortable event to unfold. That usually leads to cold sweats and eventually outright fear. The memory comes flooding back to her like a flashback from a recent war as Wendy tells the story and she's becoming a little more animated.

As husbands often do, her husband had made the decision to carry absolutely nothing. Wendy noted that they were carrying two suitcases and a bag that could have been used for a carry-on had it not been full of things that could not be carried on, like sunscreen, hair gel, etc. In her husband's mind, after careful planning, his hands would be free once the checked baggage was taken care of. However, as we all know, the vision that we so carefully construct is often hijacked once the plan is in motion!

It was their turn to stand at the counter in front of the young, over exuberant flight attendant. "Please put two bags on the scale," the young man said. They did. Their bags were overweight . . . by 17.2 pounds! The third bag was weighed and it came in under the limit, so the challenge was to shuffle 17.2 pounds worth of "things" between the three bags so that any two would be under the limit. My friend is becoming still more animated as she relates her story. "I asked the attendant if he couldn't weigh all three bags." He responded, "No ma'am, we have our rules." As she is relating the story, Wendy turns to me in exasperation and says, "Does that make any sense to you? Aren't all the bags going on the same plane?" Well, she *does* have a point! Come to think of it, no matter how the suitcases are shuffled, the overall weight of the passengers and luggage is going to be constant. It must mean something to somebody.

So they set about shuffling their worldly goods around. Fortunately, they had an extra beach bag and it became the recipient of much of the extra weight. Once the shuffling had been completed under the watchful eye of other passengers, who were probably by now reaching for their own anxiety pills, the suitcases were weighed again. "Ma'am, you are 1.8 pounds overweight." Wendy looked around for the woman who had shuffled her tiny shorts to ask for advice. Finally, she asked, "How much would it cost us to pay for the extra?" The attendant said, "$140." "You have got to be (insert adjective) kidding me," Wendy said as they set about one more time to find a balance. Finally, after doing the suitcase shuffle for what seemed an interminable amount of time, they were given their boarding passes and sent to the next point of frustration and anxiety . . . Security.

I had the vision in my head of two slightly humiliated and hugely disgruntled passengers as they trudged through the airport, each now with a carry-on destined for the inside of the airplane. He who had so carefully planned so as to be carry-on free was now trudging along with a beach bag laden with most of the 17.2 pounds of overflow, including snorkel gear, flip flops, and other paraphernalia. And who was waiting for them at the gate to take their boarding passes? The same officious little bast . . . er, I mean, attendant! Wendy said that she rewarded him with a huge smile that could have been interpreted any number of ways, but that was really intended to convey one emotion.

In the end, it may have been the attendant who won this particular battle. When Wendy and her husband got on the plane for their week-long second honeymoon, they discovered that they had been given boarding passes with seats that were rows apart. However, Wendy said it might have been a blessing in disguise as it gave her a chance to cool down about her husband's initial decision not to carry anything on the plane.

But the second round also went to the attendant. When Wendy and her husband arrived in Cuba and talked to some people, they found out that the other people also had too much luggage. "How much were you overweight?"

"About 4.5 pounds."

"And how much did you have to pay?" The reply did not help to defuse the situation. They were charged $10 for roughly the same amount of extra weight for which Wendy and her husband were told they'd have to pay $140! Somewhere, an officious little flight attendant is smiling and counting the bonus cash he is taking from unsuspecting passengers who just want to get to their destinations.

The only positive outcome of Wendy's story was that they weren't hassled at Security. But we've been there and have our own little experiences we'd like to share.

14

NO ONE *WANTS* to say that their anxiety level has increased since 9/11, but I think everyone *has* to say their anxiety level has increased since 9/11. We had booked a flight before 9/11 occurred and we found ourselves on an airplane a few days after it happened. Of course, the first thing that pops into your head is that the last thing you will see is the Sears Tower in Chicago! There was some comfort as we settled into our seats. The last person to get on the plane was huge! And he was wearing a jacket on a hot day! And he was supposedly a flight attendant but he could barely squeeze between the rows. In some strange way, the sight of that huge man, sweating in a jacket that appeared to bulge slightly on one side, delivering coffee as he made his way sideways down the rows between the seats brought a sense of calm among the passengers that day.

It's quite amazing how things changed on 9/11. I don't know about you, but I check out everyone on the aircraft. Everyone is under suspicion until proven innocent. As the plane is making its way across the skies, I check those in the immediate vicinity to see what they're up to. I don't care what complexion their skin is; I'm checking them out!

For that reason, the security check has become a necessary evil and another source of frustration in this seemingly endless journey before the journey. Off with your shoes, off with your belt, and off with your head if you are carrying any liquid beyond the agreed-upon standard set by the airline industry. If you're lucky, you won't have to display everything in the full body scanner. It isn't the fact they are scanning your body. It's the snickers you can hear coming from behind the curtain as they closely examine every part of your body that could be carrying concealed weapons or contraband of some sort.

Ron the Cowboy eventually learned to pack his belt and its giant buckle in his carry-on luggage. Nevertheless, he has been singled out on more than one occasion. One time through Security it was a shiny object in his carry-on that attracted the guard's interest. "Could it be a mirror?" Ron isn't one to be carrying a mirror so the answer was an emphatic, "No!" After the mandatory opening of the case to examine the contents, the security agent was able to find the offending shiny object. It was the back of the belt buckle lying there benignly among his other belongings.

As he points out, though, perhaps his most interesting moment with Security came on one of the first trips when he wore the belt buckle and a shirt with many, many silver buttons. The rest of us had come through Security with no problem and Ron was bringing up the rear. Every available alarm went off and security guards came running from all directions. We all stood and watched as he was ordered to remove his hat and boots, roll up his sleeves, and undo the buttons on his shirt down to the top of his jeans. The wand was passed over him and it emitted its little shriek.

Then the belt came off, the shirt was pulled out of his pants, and the last button was undone. The wand shrieked. Then he had to undo his pants and open the top. The wand still shrieked. Finally, he was told to sit down. So there he sat with no hat or shoes, with his sleeves rolled up to the elbow, and his shirt undone and hanging outside his pants, which were also hanging open. He was in the middle of the hallway with security guards conferring all around him as passengers streamed by. Ron being Ron, he looked very relaxed with a big goofy grin on his face, occasionally smiling and nodding at fellow travellers. Finally, the guards decided that this guy from western Canada, who wasn't the least bit embarrassed, and who was just patiently waiting until everyone around him came to their senses, couldn't possibly be a threat to anyone. The guards are probably wondering to this day what was still setting off the alarms after Ron disrobed. Perhaps it was the residual from his belt buckle.

There've been special moments for me in front of this final bastion protecting us from the bad guys. There was the security agent in Tanzania, Africa, who claimed I had liquids in my carry-on luggage. "No, I don't," I assured him. "Yes, you do," he said. "No, I DON'T!" I was thinking that this was descending into a struggle for domination between two eight-year-olds. Just as emphatically he insisted that I did indeed have liquids. "Why don't you check," I strongly suggested. "Just get out of here," he said without checking my luggage. I still wonder what that was all about. Bizarre!

It got a little worse in Turkey when I accidently brushed against the side of the ancient security scanner. It immediately shut down and I was obviously in big trouble for touching it. In spite of the ministrations of a number of personnel, they just could not get that scanner going. They finally told us to proceed, and we told them that hundreds of people destined for the same cruise ship as us were coming behind us. Last we saw they were working feverishly on the machine with hoards of travellers descending upon them. While his co-workers worked on the machine, the formerly friendly gentleman who initially checked us through had transformed into the Incredible Hulk, green and perspiring, and was shooting daggers at me with his eyes as we quickly made our way around the corner and out of sight.

A similar situation arose when I went through Security at the U.S. Embassy in Ottawa. I had forgotten that my cellular phone was in my pocket. When I went through the scanner, the security guard asked nicely if I had anything in my pocket. I didn't think I did and I answered accordingly. He said, "Well, actually you do." I looked again and sheepishly pulled my phone out of my pocket. I was happy that it was the tolerant team that was on duty at that particular moment.

Brenda describes an incident that occurred when they were on a trip to South Africa.

"We took a flight from Johannesburg to Dakar. At Dakar, security personnel literally tore the plane apart while we remained on board for two hours. Each of us had to remain in our assigned seat with our carry-on luggage on our laps while the security staff removed the head rests. We each only got to stand as our seat cushions were removed. The noises below us told us that the luggage was being removed and rechecked.

"After Security was certain that the plane was secure, the new passengers were allowed to board. The seats were so close together that my knees were touching the seat in front of me. I am five feet tall. You can imagine what it was like for some of the people who were six feet tall or more.

"We were finally on our way to New York, after which we had to clear Customs, travel by bus to the next terminal, go through Security again, and catch a flight to Toronto. After going through Customs again in Toronto, we were on our way home by air. It was forty-eight hours from the time we left South Africa until we were finally in bed!"

Evelyn and I also experienced a forty-eight-hour journey from Arusha, Tanzania, to our home. On the final leg from Detroit, the staff at the desk decided that, somehow, we weren't in the system. I went and sat down in disgust. Evelyn stood beside the desk with a very forlorn look on her face, eyes on the verge of bursting into tears, and the clerk finally assured her that we would get on the airplane. We did.

When we fly, we have to go when and where the airplanes go. Once on board, there are other issues to deal with. Turbulence brings a whole new level of fear. Three things happen. There is the first bump, followed immediately by the seat belt sign lighting up and then by the announcement that is barely audible saying something about flying to a higher altitude to try to avoid the impending roller coaster ride. It rarely works in my experience. Or, if it does, I would hate to think what it would have been like had we not gone to a higher altitude. The airplane rocks and rolls, dips and dives, and you close your eyes and quietly thank the workers and designers who put the thing together. How do those wings stay on when they are bouncing like that? I don't know. I am just glad they do.

The carts are quickly rolled out of sight to avoid injury. What a disappointment. I was really looking forward to my bag of peanuts. Oh, just a second, that unfortunate little boy six rows back is allergic to peanuts so anyone six rows in front and six rows behind cannot have any. Does anyone know why the airline would serve peanuts when so many people have violent allergic reactions to them? I don't. Whatever happened to pretzels?

Brenda jumps into the conversation again to announce that there is one issue that hasn't been addressed yet. I think, surely we can't beat up the airline industry more than we already have. But apparently we can.

"Jim and I were at Livingstone Airport in Zambia with a group of forty-four other people going through the security check after getting our boarding passes. We noticed that one member of our group was taking an unusually long time at the desk obtaining her pass. Another member of our group went back to see what the problem was and, as she listened to the conversation, it became apparent that our friend was being told there were no more seats available on the plane. Furthermore, she would have to wait for the next flight, which was going out maybe later that day or maybe not 'til late the next day.

"Our friend was adamant that she was not staying in Zambia and that she was going to continue the journey with everyone else in the group. Finally, the airline clerk hand wrote a boarding pass for her, and she was allowed to pass through Security and board the plane. All seemed to be well and she was relieved until she searched for her seat. It turned out her seat number was the number for the toilet!

"She was dumbstruck and panicking! 'Is there a seat belt for that toilet?' On the verge of bursting into tears, as many people do when dealing with the airlines, she was finally assured by the stewardess that there might be one seat available in first class. There was a painful waiting period as all passengers had to board before the final decision was made, but her wait was rewarded with a first class seat from Zambia to South Africa."

After a few flights, you become an expert in flying, although the closest you ever came was building a model airplane. You turn to your neighbour as the airplane makes its descent and quietly whisper, just loud enough so that he can hear, "The pilot is coming in too fast." Then Captain Kangaroo manages to bounce off the tarmac a couple of times, just before slamming on the brakes and making a violent turn toward the gate. You turn to your neighbour again and, with a satisfied look on your face, you mumble, "See, I told you he was coming in too fast!"

Yes, life as a traveller has changed . . . and not for the better. The folks who work for the airlines do the best they can under stressful conditions and, usually, we get to where we're going with a few more stories to tell. We just have to keep reminding ourselves that it's the destination that really matters!

In spite of having to endure these issues with air travel, it's exciting to travel to a new destination, and when it's a resort area where the goal is to just sit back and watch the world go by, the destination really does matter. We have all had the good fortune to experience resort living and we are about to discuss the pros and cons of being pampered for a week or two, though we might have some difficulty finding any cons.

15

GETTING AWAY for a few days in a warmer clime is reinvigorating to say the least. Coming back to a cold climate with a suntan can make you forget that the groundhog predicted six more weeks of winter. But it's tough sometimes. I've never tried it but I think it's fair to say that even chaining oneself to a street lamp and pretending to have a nervous breakdown probably won't guarantee an extension of your stay in the nice warm sun.

It's a nice break while it lasts. The suntan often fades before there's time to show it off, or at the very least before the last credit card charge is paid. People in Canada like to go to warmer climates for the winter, even if it's just for a week. When winter lasts for six months of the year and it happens year after year, there comes a point when it's time to search for warmer climates. There's resort-style living, which clearly has its advantages and there are other sunny options, like going to Las Vegas, Florida, Hawaii, or Portugal for a week or two.

One of the first opportunities for Evelyn and me to experience fun in the sun was Viva Las Vegas! In a survey done in 2005, Las Vegas was determined to have the second most popular nickname in the United States after "The Big Apple." Of course, that nickname is "Sin City." My personal favourite is "The Big Easy" (New Orleans) but no one asked me. Las Vegas did garner top honours for its slogan, which is, "What happens here stays here." That slogan has been adapted everywhere else around the world to, "What happens in Vegas stays in Vegas."

I decide to break that code here and let the group in on a couple of secrets. "Since Las Vegas is known as Sin City, you're probably expecting something salacious, right? If that's the case, sorry, but you should have bought an erotic novel like *Beautiful Tractors and the Men Who Love Them*." (That is my little shot at the farmers in the room.) There will be no gratuitous sexual anecdotes at this juncture of the conversation. I am sure the story would be more sensational if I talk about the mirrored ceiling (here we go again) over the four-poster bed in our room at Caesar's Palace. But since my wife is sitting beside me, I fear she will accuse me of exaggerating or make some comment like, "Who were you with? That didn't happen when I was there." Either way, I decide to stick to the facts we can agree on.

Evelyn and I have visited Las Vegas twice. The first time we paid our own way, rode a bus from Los Angeles, and stayed in a fleabag motel off the strip. To give you an idea of when we were there, if we had thought of it soon enough, we could have bought tickets to see Elvis! By the time we decided to go, we were able to get tickets to see the Captain and Tennille, Neil Sedaka, and Larry Storch. Google them! They do exist.

Larry Storch probably gave the audience the best advice that anyone could ever receive in that city. I'm paraphrasing, but he said something to the effect that a gambler should leap on the table, swallow all the black $100 chips, eat some prunes, and wait for nature to take its course. It's probably the only way to win!

I thought I had the answer. I read two books about playing craps and set aside $35 to lose every day. That was a relatively significant amount of money for us in those days. Craps is a game of dice where you bet on the outcome of the roll. Because I "knew what I was doing," I was full of confidence and ready to come home with a fortune. The only craps table I could find was at Caesar's, and the only table I could find had a $5 minimum bet. I lost my $35 in about five minutes on each of the first two days! I had to veer from the strategy I learned in the book and I did it drastically. So much for being an expert! The next logical step perhaps would have been to take Larry Storch's advice, but I was happy enough playing the slots for the rest of the week. I took Evelyn's advice and went down the street with her to play the penny slots.

The second visit was a business trip. That is how we got to stay at Caesar's Palace where the conference was being held. When we arrived, we expected to see Romans in chariots waiting for us. Well, what do you know! There were some. At least they were dressed like Romans. And they may not have had chariots but they were standing around looking as if their chariots would be arriving any minute. And, for a small price, we could have our picture taken with them!

It was a magnificent place back then. It probably still is. We travelled with my boss and his wife and had adjoining rooms. We were visiting their room, and he would nip into their kitchenette to make the worst Bloody Marys we had ever tasted. They were appropriately named because like Mary, Queen of Scots, we lost our bloody heads every time we drank a few. Poor Mary! She lost *her* head, but that *will* teach her to marry her first cousin!

Evelyn had the right response to the Bloody Marys. She would disappear every few minutes into our room when another round showed up. She later confided that she was dumping them down the sink in our room. I was wondering where her new-found capacity for drink came from!

While my boss and I attended the conference sessions, Evelyn and my boss's wife enjoyed a spousal package, touring Las Vegas, including a presentation by the Rockettes and a real estate tour. My boss and I left one of the more boring lectures at the conference a little early to scope out the surroundings. As most people know, Caesar's Palace is famous for holding championship boxing matches, and a ring happened to be set up in the area behind the hotel. There wasn't anyone around, so we had the brilliant idea of getting up in the ring so that we could later brag about it to our buddies. As it turned out, we weren't completely alone as a voice rang out, "Hey, ged oudda da ring." What!?? "Ged oudda da ring wid your shoes on! Youse'll get inta trouble!" Okay, we got out of the ring, and this extremely muscular, good-looking young man came up to us and started talking. We introduced ourselves and he did likewise. He told us his name and said that he had sparred with Cassius Clay (Muhammad Ali for the younger crowd). We said how nice that was for him, talked a little more, and went on our way, smirking over having actually been in the ring at Caesar's and been kicked out by some guy who had himself convinced that he had actually sparred with Cassius Clay.

I GUESS WE MISSED THE BOAT

About two weeks later, I was settling onto the couch on a Saturday afternoon to see what I could find on TV. I found something all right. The scene was the ring at Caesar's Palace where we had stood and the event was the lightweight championship of the world. One of the contenders was the young man who had kicked us out of the ring.

I admit I exaggerated the way he spoke (as my wife said I would about the mirror, proving once again that she is always right). He was a polite young man and very well spoken. He didn't win the match that I watched that day but he later went on to become the World Boxing Association Lightweight Champion. His name was Ray "Boom Boom" Mancini.

Evelyn and my boss and his wife had to fly out a day before I was scheduled to go, for various reasons. I decided to spend my day at the pool. There was a manmade island in the middle with a series of indentations where swimmers could rest their necks. I did that while the waiters and waitresses waded out to where I was lying with my drink of choice. The water lapped over my body occasionally, just enough to cool me off, and it was just a tremendously peaceful place to be.

What I didn't realize was that the temperature had soared to 103 degrees Fahrenheit in the shade. I could lie there all day and I almost did. When I returned to the room (okay, I will let everyone into the room for this story) and removed my bathing suit, I could not believe how burned I was! The contrast between the skin on my legs where my bathing suit was and the skin on my legs where my bathing suit wasn't was shocking. I was broiled! Lobster, anyone?

That night I could not stand anything on my legs, and the airplane ride home the next day was by far the most uncomfortable one I have ever had. And airplane rides are not known for their comfort. But you know the amazing thing? I didn't peel, the pain went away, and to this day my legs darken quicker than the rest of my body. I think I dodged a bullet. At least I hope I did.

In spite of the sunburn, there's something to be said for just resting and relaxing with no particular agenda. We'll have to try that some more!

16

WE ALL TOOK A FEW more trips individually before we became part of the travelling group gathered here today. Ed and Carol are telling us about their trip to a resort in Mexico. As they disembarked from the airplane, they were met by hordes of uniformed people offering tours, excursions, and other delights to introduce the unsuspecting tourists to their country. "In fact," Ed says, "it was so difficult to fight our way through the crowd that we missed our bus!" There they were, stranded in a foreign country! As I have described him earlier, Ed is a distinguished-looking gentleman with white wavy hair and white bushy eyebrows. He is the tallest of the group and he has a slight build. All of that seems to be to his advantage when he turns into Ed the Negotiator. Seeing him transform is like watching Superman donning his cape. He takes on a charisma that transforms him from "just Ed" to Ed the Negotiator.

He hailed a taxi and gave the driver the name of the hotel. "Okay, no problem, *señor*! Sixty-five dollars!" Even in this situation in a foreign country with very few options, Ed had the gumption to negotiate! "Thirty-five," he said. There's a lesson here. Even though you have no clue where you are going or how long it will take and therefore no concept of what the cost should be, whatever the driver says is probably too much. It's worth trying to dicker. The worst thing they can say to you is "no." It's always worth a try.

They agreed on middle ground and climbed into the taxi to head off toward their hotel. The first stop as they were leaving the airport in their seven-seat "limousine" was a gate where the driver gave the gatekeeper some money. Carol pointed out that the stars weren't aligning as they should. Now they were in a foreign country, their bus had left them behind, they were in a beaten-up, seven-seat vehicle, and the driver was slipping someone some money for no apparent reason!!

As we all know, it's amazing what your mind can do, and at this point they had visions of being driven to a back alley and as a best case scenario being relieved of their valuables. The worst case scenario would see their heads and bodies being shipped home in separate boxes. "As it turned out," Ed says, "we were delivered to the right hotel and our heads remained attached to our torsos so that we could continue to travel as a unit."

Carrying on with their trip to Mexico, Ed describes an excursion to the Sierra Madres. "There is something about travelling into an area that's sixty-five million years old in a vehicle that is about forty years old. Somehow, it's the truck that seems ancient. The truck was powered by gas, and we were fuelled by tequila and beer as we sat under a canvas in the back. We arrived at a small village where tortillas were being cooked over an open fire. The tortillas tasted great, but eventually the tequila and beer took its toll and we had to use the bathroom. We discovered that the bathroom consisted of a hole in the floor and a bucket of water." At this point, Carol chimes in, "The women in the group decided they didn't have to go after all." As Ed and Carol found out on their Mexican trip, even though resort living has its advantages, the excursions can show the traveller what life is really like in the destination country.

Evelyn and I had resort-style vacations before joining the group as well. We visited Cayo Coco in Cuba on our first all-inclusive vacation. Little did we know that charter aircraft take the discomfort of air travel to an entirely new level. Take a small, old aircraft and add a few rows of seats. It is only a four-hour flight. None of these dumb tourists will notice that their knees are planted firmly in front of their noses. Nobody will pass out because of lack of air in the cabin. They're all too excited about going and they will all be too hung over when they come back to even notice. Evelyn and I are not tall people, and our knees were placed firmly in front of our noses *before* the person in front of us, no doubt a member of the "Me" generation, had the temerity to put his seat back. One unfortunate young man who was well over six feet tall really did pass out from the ordeal. You'd think the seats would be prevented from being put back when there is no room to start with!

As the airplane was starting its final approach into the airport in Cuba, I felt that same urge that Ed and Carol had in Mexico. I had to use the facilities. *We will soon be on the ground,* I thought! I can wait. As we landed, there were army personnel with machine guns there to greet us and usher us into a small waiting room. We were stuck at the back of the crowd and there was one Customs officer present. The army officers were busy checking out the new chiquitas who had arrived with us.

As we stood there waiting for our turn at Customs, my urge became considerably more urgent, if you know what I mean. I decided I had to pry one of the officer's eyes away from the girls long enough to escort me to where I needed to go. Finally, one of them reluctantly looked my way and I asked if he could point me to the bathroom. "No comprendo," he said gruffly. "BATH ROOM," I said louder, hoping that would somehow make him understand. Incredibly, he seemed to get it because he motioned as if he was peeing. "Yes," I said. He hoisted his gun onto his shoulder, beckoned me to follow him, which I dutifully did, and we made our way through the crowd and out a side door to a bathroom. He patiently stood guard like a Buckingham Palace sentry while I went. Then we repeated the process back through the crowd.

It's a long, slow ride through the countryside and sights of some of the worst poverty imaginable to a little piece of paradise. What a contrast! But, if you can stand the journey, the destination is kind of fun. The Cuban beaches are of soft, white sand like fine sugar sitting in a bowl. The water is a beautiful blue colour and the days are idyllic. People are having a great time. The resort is alive with the calypso beat, and with a rolled up American dollar bill or two every time you buy a drink, the bartenders quickly remember your name and your beverage of choice when you wander up to one of the many bars. Since the drinks are included, many of the tourists spend the first two days staggering down the beach after consuming too many pina coladas and then they disappear for the rest of the week into their rooms to nurse a massive hangover and cruel sunburn.

Evelyn and I consumed our fair share of pina coladas and *cervezas* (beer) respectively in the first two days or so. Evelyn had been working hard before we left, and the combination of drinks and sun quickly took their toll. She fell sound asleep in the room. I would go back periodically and, like any good husband, I held a mirror under her nose to make sure she was still breathing. She woke up completely refreshed after her sixteen-hour nap and she was ready to go. However, we discovered one thing on that trip that we hadn't thought of previously. In the sunshine and heat, I tend to be energized. For Evelyn it's the opposite. We will have to remember that!

It's fun to observe the people. They strut and flaunt their assets in the skimpiest of bathing suits. One young lady in a stunning white thong bikini strutted up and down the beach constantly for the first day or two, chatting animatedly with her friend and tossing her hair about, until her butt cheeks turned a bright red colour. We didn't see so much of her after that. I suspect that sitting down would have been an issue for the remainder of the week. Unfortunately for her, we suspected she didn't get exactly what she had come to Cuba for. Or, maybe she did and that's why we didn't see her again!

The battle of the plastic beach chairs is an amusing sideline to anything else that one might want to do on a beach in the Caribbean. Arriving early on the beach you will find it virtually deserted, save for the plastic lounge chairs that are arrayed like so many drunken tourists. The parts of the chairs that are visible are as white as many of the travellers arriving from the snowy north for their vacation. But first thing in the morning, they are adorned with a dazzling array of colourful beach items. Cover-ups are draped on the chairs here, beach towels are draped on the chairs over there, and beach bags adorn still others. It is a potpourri of beach things, colourfully flaunting themselves in the shade of the sign that blares, "NO RESERVING CHAIRS." Apparently, brains take some time to thaw out after they come down from the frozen north.

We met two young girls, Emily and Sarah, from Canada, who pretty much adopted us. They were on their first trip together and they would seek us out to tell us about their day and ask for advice. They were a bit naive but smart enough to seek help in a foreign country. One day, they decided they would go skydiving. Sarah, who was the more adventurous of the two, was very excited. Emily was a little more reserved and obviously nervous. So were we.

We had virtually adopted these girls as well in the short time we had known them. They were to get into a Cuban airplane and land by parachute on the beach in tandem with an expert. Now you've probably heard the question about why anyone in their right mind would jump out of a perfectly good airplane. Well, in this case, I was worried that the Cuban aircraft would not be perfectly good and that maybe the girls would be smart to jump out, provided that the parachute was perfectly good. We watched the airplane circle overhead, and two tiny specks emerged from the door. As they plummeted toward the ground, we grew a little more agitated. But finally, the parachutes puffed open, and there they were silhouetted against the blue sky drifting toward their landing place on the hot white sand.

They landed perfectly and after thanking their tandem riders, they rushed over to tell us about their experience. Sarah was alive with excitement; her eyes were sparkling, and we sensed that it wouldn't be long until she jumped out of an airplane again. Emily's eyes were alive, too . . . with shock and a severe adrenaline rush. Her fair skin was even paler and she was shivering from the experience, but she was very proud of herself for having survived the challenge of facing a fear head on and winning.

Emily had been telling us since we met them how much she disliked wine. That night as we sat outside at a table with the ocean breeze rustling the palm fronds overhead, the waves gently rolling in, and the brilliant moonlight illuminating our surroundings, the girls approached us after a celebratory dinner. They were a little tipsy and as they approached we could see that Emily had a half full wine glass in her hand. She proclaimed with a giggle, "I love wine!" We weren't sure what to make of it. Perhaps she was celebrating having survived the jump or she had simply been encouraged by Sarah to again try something different. We're not sure if her new-found "love" of wine endured beyond the shores of the island as we haven't seen or heard from them since.

We decided we wanted to experience Cuba a little, and as with any all-inclusive, there are excursions at an extra cost that relieve you of your money and are often of questionable value. There was a bus trip into a typical Cuban town called Moron (pronounced Moroan), and we thought it would be a good way to get to see what Cuba was really like, although we had seen it briefly on the way from the airport. We had a guide who told us about the history of Cuba and who blamed most of their problems on the embargo.

As we crossed a bridge, we noticed a truck full of workers had left the road and was half submerged upside down in the water. Some of the workers were sitting sadly by the side of the road with their heads down, and one or two were diving into the water to salvage whatever they could. Some of the tourists on our bus laughed at the sight, but I guess they didn't realize that it was a tragedy for the people of very limited means who owned the truck and for those who were trying to get to work. We all have a different sense of what is funny and, unfortunately, a widely differing capacity to imagine the lives of others.

As we drove into town, we passed a blue three-storey building with few windows. The windows that were there were broken or cracked. The building was dilapidated and decrepit. It was a sad remnant of its former self as it must have stood there in splendour at one time in its history. We couldn't imagine that anyone would live there now. We moved on into town, and when the bus stopped, it was immediately surrounded by kids asking for handouts. Evelyn and I were wearing baseball hats that they wanted. One of them proudly proclaimed, "Toronto Blue Jays." That appeared to be all the English he knew. If you give something to one, you have to give something to all and we were sorry we hadn't come prepared. That's a lesson for next time.

We were driven around town in a horse-drawn buggy and shown the sites of Moron. It's a very poor town, and we were told that most of the people who work at Cayo Coco live in Moron. One of the most interesting sites was a giant rooster statue that dominates the town. We felt that we were the ones on display as we made our way past earthen floor houses, and the many residents stared as we passed.

That night at dinner, we chatted with the waitress. She asked what we did that day, and we told her that we had gone to see Moron. Her eyes lit up, and she asked if we saw a blue apartment building. We said we had. She said, "That's where I live. You like?" We were momentarily struck dumb and, finally, our simple answer was, "Yes, it's nice." She was very proud of her home and we realized that home is what you make it.

There are some beautiful restaurants at the resort, dedicated to a variety of food. We decided to go to the seafood restaurant for a special meal one evening. Once again, the ocean breeze was blowing through the open air restaurant, we were dressed as well as we could be given the vacation style clothing we had brought, and we were sharing a nice bottle of wine and enjoying quiet conversation. It was relatively early in the evening, and the moon's rays were bouncing off the waves as they gently rolled in. Surprisingly, we were the only ones in the restaurant and the waiters were not in any hurry to serve us. Then we understood why. The noise of a machine could be heard coming along the path toward the restaurant.

It was getting louder and louder, and having grown up on the farm, I knew the unmistakable sounds of a tractor. It was a small tractor, but a tractor nonetheless. The noise pollution was immediately followed by air pollution as a wave of pesticide wafted through the restaurant. There would be no bugs in the restaurant that evening and no dinner either. Note to selves: go to dinner later next time so that we could at least pretend the food hadn't been sprayed. What we don't know won't kill us. Will it?

A second excursion offered a boat ride adventure through the rainforest. I have always had a fascination with the rainforest, and we thought this might be a way of seeing it up close and personal without the bug bites. We were ushered on to a high-powered boat along with other unsuspecting passengers by a young Cuban. Once we were seated near the back of the boat beside the driver, he looked at Evelyn, turned his hat backwards, smiled a cocky little smile, and wound the throttle around as far as it would go.

If you have ever seen a rocket launch on television, you will have noticed that, when the countdown reaches zero, enormous plumes of fuel vapours are jettisoned for a few seconds as the rocket quivers on its launch pad until it finally starts to move. It was something like that. Fortunately, no one fell out of the boat as it stood on end like a wild mustang with its two front legs pawing the air. It was as if it was straining against some unseen barrier until it finally broke the imaginary tether and we rocketed across the lagoon.

We headed straight for a post, that was sticking out of the water, and as we veered around it, I thought I heard the driver with the throttle in his hand laughing manically beside us. We made it to the other side of the lake in minutes, and our heart rates started to return to normal as we slowly cruised through the rainforest as the wake of our passage still rolled across the water. There were a few minutes of relative peace as we coasted through the flora. The driver had turned his hat forward as we meandered through the shaded beauty of the lush green wonderland with its branches hanging within touching distance.

Then it was time to go as our Cuban Mario Andretti turned his hat backwards once again. He looked at Evelyn with that cheeky grin, which grew even wider when she turned *her* hat backwards, and we put a death grip on the edges of the boat. Once again we flew across the lake, leaving a trail of thunder echoing across the water and a cloud of exhaust behind us. When we arrived safely back at the dock, we disembarked and returned to the safety of our home away from home to collect our thoughts. Most of us were exhilarated by the experience and excited to have arrived back at the dock in one piece. But one woman was heard to exclaim to our driver and guide, "Thank you very much for scaring the shit out of me." He shrugged as if he didn't understand a word and waited patiently for the next batch of victims.

Of course, when in Cuba, you have to go snorkeling. The water is clear and calm and tourists are just drawn to it like a nail to a magnet. We decided to go on an organized snorkeling excursion and, undeterred by our last boating experience, we waded through the shallows to climb into another boat to make our way out into the ocean to snorkel. As we waded out, a woman said to our guide that she heard there were snakes in the water. He said, "No, missus, the snakes don't come out until eleven o'clock." He turned away and rolled his eyes. Man, these tourists are idiots!

We picked up a few other tourists at another resort where the jellyfish appeared to outnumber the paying customers. It's an eerie feeling to touch a jellyfish in the water, and we didn't welcome the prospect of someone peeing on a sting to relieve the pain (as I've been led to believe actually works) so I was pleased we were not staying there. As we made our way out to the middle of the ocean, the water got deeper and deeper but it was quite clear. It must have been incredibly clear to our guide as his high definition eyes picked up something on the bottom of the ocean and he yelled to our driver to stop the boat. He dove into the water and came up with a star fish. We all held it and marvelled at this beautiful sea creature and wondered how such a thing could actually be a living marine animal. I wondered something else. Maybe I am suspicious by nature, but as everyone congratulated our guide for his incredibly keen eyesight for being able to spot a star fish in thirty feet of water from the front of a moving boat, I wondered how he could possibly have done it. "Enjoy the moment," Evelyn said as she patted my knee, and I settled back, waiting for our swimming adventure . . . with more than a little trepidation.

Now, I had snorkeled before, but it was by walking out far enough to swim. This was our first experience with actually being told in the middle of the ocean, "Okay, go!" I firmly believe the tour operators had no clue how many of us were on that boat as we got to choose our snorkels and goggles from a barrel. However, there was no danger of us being left behind as we didn't stay in the water that long. I'm not a great swimmer and I wasn't particularly comfortable with thirty feet of water underneath me. Nor would I have been comfortable with thirty feet of water over my head. The only thing we could see in any direction was our boat. Evelyn is a strong swimmer but she got out early as well. As we made our way back to shore, I hoped that no one had been shark bait that day.

The most notable thing about Cuba is the beaches. The resorts are apart from the rest of the world. The island appears to be beautiful and not overly busy (at least when we were there). Of course, lurking behind the beauty is extreme poverty and we should never forget that. It doesn't hurt to take some extra toothpaste and other basic necessities to share with the locals. The people who work at the resorts are the lucky ones. They are employed and receive a regular income, although I'm not sure how well paid they are. There are many who are not employed and merely existing.

But we did like resort living and Evelyn and I decided to try an all-inclusive vacation again. This time we hopped aboard an overcrowded airplane and headed for one of Christopher Columbus's great discoveries, the Dominican Republic, or the DR as it is known to us know-it-alls.

17

IT WAS PUNTA CANA, land of palm trees, beautiful beaches, and topless French Canadian sun worshippers from Quebec. In spite of the fact that some of the latter were moving into their twilight years, there were many breasts exposed on the beaches of the DR. In fact, as some of them were lying on their backs, you had to be very careful where you walked. Gravity gets all of us, eventually.

Of course, the beaches are indescribable once again and the resort is opulent. But as always seems to happen, another interesting incident occurred in the life of these intrepid travellers, this time in the surf at the DR. I was enjoying the waves with the sun pouring down. The waves were crashing in to shore and then retreating back out toward the ocean only to repeat over and over as they have been doing for millions of years. There was the outline of people visible parasailing in the brilliant sky and young males on the beach hawking rides on tricycles with giant surf wheels. The beach was alive with the sound of people having fun, and as I looked back toward the beach without my glasses, every imaginable colour and style of bathing attire melded together into a splash of magnificence, dominating the sand. I could feel the gentle tug of the undertow, trying to drag the swimmers back out to sea to join the fishes. I often wondered if there is anything to the theory that the seventh wave is the best one for surfers, and at what point do you start the count?

I had put the key to our room safe in the pocket of my bathing suit. We were aware that the next day we would be leaving for our snowy climate back home so we were making the most of every moment on the beach. Then it happened! A large wave (maybe it was the seventh) came crashing in and turned me upside down. It was exhilarating, and I was laughing

I GUESS WE MISSED THE BOAT

as I staggered back out to the beach to lie in the sun, catch my breath, and dry off for a while.

I put my glasses back on; we gathered our things and went back to the room. I dug for the key in my bathing suit pocket so we could open the safe containing our passports, whatever remaining cash we had, and other valuables. No key!! In the topsy-turvy experience in the waves, the key must have dropped out of my pocket. Now what!!?? We went to the front desk in the main building and explained the situation. Three times. The desk manager said in an almost unintelligible mixture of English and Spanish, "Thees is veerry bad." What? "Thees is veerry bad, sir." Oh! He called another manager, someone more senior, apparently, who came and explained that this was indeed very bad. Well, we knew it was very bad but what are we going to do about it? We have to leave in the morning; we have no passports. I could see dollar signs flashing through my head as we were in the DR in an extremely vulnerable position. This IS very bad!

The manager explained that there were no extra keys anywhere in Punta Cana and no one capable of cutting keys, so a new one would have to be cut somewhere else. It would require a flight to Santo Domingo and it would take all day . . . if we were lucky! The dollar signs were spinning in my head like the symbols on the slot machines we had played in Las Vegas. A flight to Santo Domingo, all day, this could cost thousands. But it must be done. We have to get home.

He told us to come back in a few hours. What was that about enjoying our last day on the beach? The wait was agonizing! Finally, we decided to go back to the lobby, and the clerk said that the person was not back from Santo Domingo but that we should wait there. He said this was very bad. We waited and waited and waited. Finally, we were told to report to the desk. I asked how much it would be. I didn't realize it, but my hands were clenching the desk and probably leaving an indentation of my finger prints. I was sweating profusely and my knees were weak.

He said, "I am very sorry, sir, but this is very bad. It will cost you $50." I nearly fainted! Really!!?? I couldn't wait to pay in case there was some mistake and said I would be happy to pay as soon as we could GET SOME MONEY FROM THE SAFE! All of a sudden, out of nowhere a maintenance man showed up with a new lock for the safe. We went to the room, he took out the old one, put in the new one (all in about thirty seconds), and we were saved. In the end, it wasn't so bad and I learned to tie the key to my bathing suit next time.

The airplane ride back from the DR proved interesting as the plane does a loop from the freezing cold climate in Canada to the very warm climate in the Caribbean and back again. The air conditioning causes condensation to form on the ceiling of the aircraft, and as water tends to do, it will run wherever it wants and, as the plane is taking off, it will drip on one of the unsuspecting passengers. If having some liquid drip on you from the ceiling of an aircraft doesn't raise your level of anxiety on a flight, it's likely that nothing will.

All-inclusive resorts are a wonderful way to vacation. You're totally free, not having to worry about time (at least for the first few days), money (unless you are going on an excursion), bugs (as we found out), the top to your bathing suit (male or female), and things that are going on at home can be completely forgotten for a while. The resort staff knows where their bread is buttered, and you will be pampered so much that you will not want to leave. You are made to feel special as the waiters and waitresses are very good at recognizing you and remembering your favourite drink. You are almost guaranteed perfect weather and ideal swimming conditions.

It's easy in a resort area to forget you're in a third world country, but that's indeed often the case. Most of the people serving and pampering you are doing it to squeak out a meager existence for their families. It seems like ideal working conditions, but they're not always treated well by some of the tourists who arrive with a sense of entitlement, having left their manners (and too often, brains) at the door. It doesn't hurt to treat the locals you run into well. They deserve a tip if they've done something that you appreciate. They treasure some of the things we take for granted, like toothpaste, soap, etc. It's satisfying to enjoy the trip; it's even more satisfying to know you've helped someone while you were there.

18

EVELYN AND I discovered that riding first class in an airplane is much more comfortable than riding in a canvas-covered truck, which Ed and Carol had the good fortune to do, although it may not be quite as good for building character. First class is not our normal ride. However, a trip to Portugal for an extended stay on a charter flight offered us first class for slightly more money, and we grabbed it. It's nice to be pampered occasionally and this was one of those times. First on the plane, all the drinks you want, comfortable seating, first off the plane, first luggage to arrive. Ah, that's the life. What's that noise? Oh yes, it's the sound of us falling back to reality!

Sometimes getting to the airport can be a challenge, as Brenda points out. Friends of theirs flew to the *south* airport, which is the international airport, on the island of Tenerife in the Canary Island chain. "When they went to pick up their rental car, they discovered that it was at the *north* airport, which is more commonly used by Spanish and Scandinavian services." Brenda advises us that Tenerife has about a million inhabitants, but it supports not one, but two airports! She continues her story. "It was dark and pouring rain, so they opted for taking a taxi to their rental villa and they would figure out how to pick up the car later. The problem was that their directions to the villa were from the north airport, and the taxi driver had no clue how to get there."

Brenda thinks it is funny that a taxi driver on an island of one million people wouldn't be able to find his way and, as she is known to do, laughs heartily.

"After stopping to ask for directions three times, the last time at a bar at two a.m., they were finally able to find the villa. The next morning, they took another cab to the car rental agency and rented a Jeep. They decided to take the top off the Jeep and had a wonderful sunny tour around the island. Finally, it was time for them to return the Jeep and take the flight home, but their plane was leaving from the south airport. They were on a busy six-lane highway on their way to the airport when Mother Nature decided to have a little fun with them and she opened the tap.

"Since there was nowhere to turn off the highway, the Jeep was flooded with water and the term 'drowned rat' to describe its human cargo was too kind. With their clothes outlining their bodies like the latest physical fitness fashion and their hair hanging down their faces like the tendrils of a clinging plant, she went to the luggage check-in and he returned the Jeep. He calmly and carefully explained that they had been soaked with the top down. The clerk understandably expressed some concern about the damp interior and the possibility of never renting out the Jeep again; he spoke to his superior in rapid-fire Spanish and, after a lengthy conversation, turned back and said with a forced smile, 'No problem, señor. We will deal with it.'"

Meanwhile, around the same time, Evelyn and I were discovering Portugal. We stayed in the town of Albufiera in the Algarve in a condo overlooking the Mediterranean. Every morning, I was able to get up and walk along the cliffs with the ocean crashing against the rocks below. Further west from my vantage point on the cliffs was a white Legoland of stacked houses and condominiums set back from the golden beaches. The cliffs rose from the water with occasional caves carved by the incessant pounding of the waves over the preceding centuries. Mother Nature's giant sand dunes, created by erosion and drift, interrupted the flat beach surface periodically. All of this was painted against a vast clear sky above and the seemingly endless sea to the south.

Every night was a feast of seafood, although as with any destination we have visited, we were also able to find pizza, American Chinese food, and, of course, that worldwide landmark, the giant golden arch of McDonald's! A rental car was included in our package, and every day was an adventure as we headed off without any real concern for when we would return. It was a good thing! While the roads are clearly named on the map, there is no such thing as a street sign! That made it a challenge, but the centre of our universe was a roundabout or traffic circle with exits clearly marked by statues of giant worms with sunglasses, dolphins, and a huge globe with a bullfighting ring behind it. Our daily trips always started with either worms, dolphins, or a map of the world.

We took excursions to Lisbon and Silves, Portugal, and Seville and the Rock of Gibraltar in Spain. We enjoyed the Barbary Macaque monkey civilization on the Rock that is proof once again that we haven't progressed far from our ancestors (if you subscribe to the theory that we are indeed descended from monkeys). In fact, apparently interaction with people is breaking down their social structure. It would be a sad day if the monkeys started acting more like people! I'm sure there are many who would agree they might be far better off living in their own world.

We saw the end of land on the western side of Portugal at St. Vincent where Christopher Columbus sailed off into what many thought would be oblivion. Massive waves roll into St. Vincent and crash spectacularly against the cliffs, forming giant clouds of foamy spray. It's a surfer's paradise! We dined in a restaurant under some rocks in Lagos, Portugal, with three-hundred-foot cliffs rising majestically above us. And we drove into a post in Lagos!

We were cautioned before we left Canada not to get into any accidents in Portugal. The deductible on insurance for a rented car can range from something like $1,500 to $4,000 so it can quickly multiply the cost of the trip, not to mention the inconvenience and potential pain that a person would have to go through. In fact, I think the last words we heard from well-meaning friends who had been to Portugal before we left for the airport were, "Whatever you do, don't get into an accident." No problem!

As many towns are in Europe, Lagos was walled to keep out the bad guys in days of old. I drove in confidently and quickly noted that every street was wide enough for one car and the traffic was one way. No problem so far. We had no idea where we were going, but this was an adventure, right? I turned right onto a narrow cobbled street that meandered uphill. This one was barely wide enough for two vehicles but still one way. We moved up the hill, but there was a truck ahead of us stopped near the top in the middle of the street. In front of it was a driverless van!

We sat patiently and waited. The car we had rented was a standard and my one foot was planted firmly on the brake, ensuring that we didn't roll back down the hill, while the other rested on the clutch. The driver ahead of us was waving his arms around and speaking rapidly in excited Portuguese. The missing truck driver remained missing and our little drama continued to hold us captive. Finally, it was determined that the missing driver was not about to return any time soon, so our cavalcade of two vehicles had to do something or we would have to spend the day there. We're not sure if an "All-Points Bulletin" had been issued yet or if the driver's photo was plastered on milk containers featuring missing people, but it remained apparent that he was somewhere other than behind the wheel of the van. Hopefully he was enjoying whatever it was he was doing.

There was a lane behind us and to our left, so the driver of the truck in front of us signalled that if I backed up he would be able to back into the lane, turn around, and squeeze by us with inches to spare. I took my foot off the brake, rolled back far enough that the truck could do just that and reapplied the brake. He turned around, squeezed by us and was on his way. His face was a mask of anger and he was muttering something with an adjective that started with "f" and sounded vaguely like English. He apparently was not a tourist with all day to complete his rounds. Time is money and all that.

Now it was my turn. I moved forward again far enough that I could back into the side lane. No problem, although I could feel the sweat building under my collar. As I moved forward, I realized that I had not given myself enough room to make the turn and I was now on the downward slope with my front bumper inches from a post. You know that problem I said I wouldn't have? Now, I had a problem.

I knew what had to be done. One foot was on the brake; one was on the clutch. For any of you who have driven a standard, you will know that my task was to keep my foot firmly on the brake, push in the clutch with the other foot, change gears into reverse, release the brake, and move my foot from the brake to the accelerator while releasing the clutch, all in less time than it takes for a snowflake to evaporate on a warm sidewalk. Or less time than it takes to blink an eye in Churchill. It didn't quite happen quickly enough! Into the post! Thump! Shit!

It was then that we noticed the two women standing there observing us as if we were the sports highlight of the week. Who needs television when you have tourists? They were standing in their aprons like umpires at a baseball game, laughing and waving their arms as if ruling that a runner had arrived safely at third. "No problem!" they laughed. Somehow I couldn't quite believe them and I had multiple dollar signs rolling like a movie reel through my head.

Using the post for leverage, I was able to back up carefully and far enough to get pointed in the right direction so we could return to our condo. I refused to look at the damage until we arrived in our parking spot about an hour and a half later. I had visions of a massive crease in the bumper and grill, of the paint being scraped off the hood, and of the imprint of the post running up the entire front of the car. With that, of course, would come the insurance costs and demerit points. When I did finally look, I found that, miraculously, the women were right. There was no dent in the bumper. In fact, the bumper had absorbed the impact and there wasn't even a scratch. I was very, very thankful. We shall from now on find a parking spot outside any walled city we happen to encounter and *walk* into the centre of town.

We did just that in the town of Silves, Portugal, where I really began to more fully understand Evelyn's love of castles. This was the beginning of what has come to be known as ABC travel. Another Bloody Castle. Silves has a castle built in 1200 AD, and Evelyn was in her element, exploring every nook and cranny. Her eyes lit up like a child's at Christmas and it was difficult to pry her away.

She explains her love of castles to the group in the room. "There's just something romantic and mysterious about them. I try to just stand and look at them, to take myself back in time and understand a little about the way of life and what it must have been like. First of all, there was always serious consideration given to their location. They are always situated on the top of a hill overlooking the countryside so that the enemy could be seen coming from any direction. They are built in such a way that guard towers always overlook the gates, and there are hidden passages that lead to who knows where, all designed for a purpose. I imagine how difficult it must have been for the women who really had no status at that time. I think of the clothing they wore. The structures and the history are fascinating to me."

I think we all ponder the possibility that Evelyn might have been Lady Guinevere, hanging around with Sir Lancelot in a previous life. I have to admit, it's kind of fun standing on the ramparts, imagining what it must have been like watching for

I GUESS WE MISSED THE BOAT

the enemy, spear in hand, feeling the heat emanating from the caldrons of oil bubbling away behind you, just waiting to be dumped on the bad guys as they approached. Probably the only thing that would have been scarier would be to be in the position of the approaching soldiers about to have boiling oil poured on them. I am very thankful to have been born where I was, when I was. The things that have been done in the name of religion!

Seeing the ancient walled cities and experiencing the culture in Portugal was a dream come true. We Westerners like to go into a restaurant, swallow our meal in two or three gulps, and get out of there to carry on with the latest emergency in our lives. Usually, we find out that the level of importance is not that high, but we still insist on finishing the meal as quickly as possible. In Portugal, the waiter or waitress brings the meal and disappears as if by magic. It's possible to sit there for hours without seeing the server again. It's intended to be a social experience that we Westerners have not learned to enjoy. We could certainly learn something from that leisurely approach to the meal. Not only would we learn to converse but we would undoubtedly have improved digestive systems.

There is a word of caution, though. That scrumptious-looking appetizer delivered to your table when you sit down is *not* complimentary. Because olive trees are plentiful in Portugal, the plate was usually laden with that delicacy and it made my mouth water. Evelyn wasn't as keen as she mentioned earlier. If you pick at them, they're yours. If you don't want to pay for them, ask that they be taken away.

For its beauty and weather, Portugal is matched closely by Hawaii on my list of favourites. Getting to Hawaii is a killer from the eastern part of North America, but once there, it's a piece of paradise. The easiest job (and probably most boring) in the world has to be that of the weather man in Hawaii who reports the same forecast virtually every day.

Monday forecast: Sunny and warm. High of 85 degrees.

Tuesday forecast: Sunny and warm. High of 85 degrees.

Wednesday forecast: Sunny and warm. Yawn! High of 85 degrees.

You get the picture. The only thing that seems to change is the size of the waves so the surfers listen to the forecast intently.

This was one of our extended family vacations so it was the eight of us who got to enjoy Hawaii. We travelled between islands by commuter plane, which is much the same as riding the city bus I described earlier. Because Evelyn has a cane, we were allowed to get on the plane first, while the others in our group had to patiently wait their turn. However, it took a few minutes for her to move along to our seats, and we could hear the thundering herd let loose from their spots in line before we arrived at the inside of the plane. It was like the running of the bulls as they thundered down the tunnel toward us, all hoping to claim a seat at the front so they could be the first off the plane.

I imagined Genghis Khan in the lead with his hoards of Mongols covered in animal fur on stampeding horses whose nostrils flared and snorted as they rode toward us, bent on pillage and plunder. But these weren't Mongols; they were businessmen in three-piece suits and women in professional attire, all with briefcases, not spears, approaching us at full speed. The logic defies me. It's like being on a three-lane highway as cars weave in and out of stop-and-go traffic to be the first in line. But if you pick out a lane jumper and watch its progress, invariably you will find it right beside you in the lane next to yours a few miles down the road.

So it is with the people racing to get the first seats on the airplane. Will they really gain that much time in the end? While we were sitting there, we could see our six comrades calmly walking by while there would be people in front and behind them with harried looks on their faces who couldn't wait to get to their seats. I suppose if the rushing business folks are commuting every day and gain a few seconds each time, over the course of a career it might amount to something. If nothing else, they should have a good dose of hypertension!

It's true what they say about Hawaii being paradise. We were fortunate enough to visit the Big Island, Oahu, Maui, and Kauai. What struck me most is the ever-changing landscape. From majestic waterfalls drifting down the hillside to soaring

I GUESS WE MISSED THE BOAT

mountains to beautiful canyons, the islands offer a myriad of contrasts. The turquoise waters roll onto the beaches. Volcanic eruptions over the years have littered the beaches with small stones. Some of the sand is literally black. If it's sandy beaches you're looking for, Cuba and the DR are hard to beat. But Hawaii with its charm, friendly people, and weather that never seems to change is another world entirely.

Every island has its own charm and wonders. We went whale watching on the Big Island and we were in for a treat. The giant humpback whales were breaching. They were lifting themselves, almost vertically, completely out of the water, and we could see their glistening bodies layered over the ever-clear Hawaii sky with the white froth bubbling in the hole in the ocean they just created. I don't know whether it's a mating ritual or display of dominance or simply to scare others away, but I do know for the handful of humans in the tiny boat lucky enough to witness the display a few hundred feet away, it was very impressive.

This was a Kodak moment if ever there was one. Everyone had their cameras out. We were all pointing them in the direction of the last breach. But there were two problems. The first is that whales move. So the site of the last breach was probably not going to be the location of the next one. However, that was not a big problem as we could spot the start of the next breach out of the corner of our eye and swing the camera over. There's one! The whale launches itself out of the water and the button is pressed on the camera! This is going to be a shot for *National Geographic*! The camera pauses for thought; the whale is in midair and is starting its descent. The whale's back in the water and CLICK, the camera finally takes the picture. We proudly arrive back home with photographic glimpses of the backs of whales and stories of witnessing the breaching that no one will ever believe.

Of course, one of the staples of the islands is the pineapple. They're sweet, tender, and juicy and have a beautiful colour. And the islanders don't appreciate them much. According to many people we talked to, we could take one, ten, a truckload, or keep hauling them out until there were no more for all they cared. I guess it's like living by an ocean and tiring of the view. Or it's like living in Italy and getting too much pizza. Or it's like working at a fast food restaurant in your youth and not being able to stand the sight of it for the rest of your life. There is such a thing as too much of a good thing.

Then there's the misunderstood coconut. While we walk among the coconut palms, the winds hiss through the fronds, inviting us to stop and watch the world go by. But not only is the coconut delicious, legend has it that it is lethal. We were told, and who are we to argue, that more people die by coconut in Hawaii than by any other cause. And not because they are poisonous. No, it's because people sit underneath seventy-five-foot coconut trees and doze off in the sunshine, only to be sent into the afterlife by a falling coconut travelling at warp speed. When coconut meets head, there is a good chance coconut will win. The same would apply to any other part of the anatomy, so the only solution seems to be to wear full body armour when walking among the coconut trees. It may be more than a little embarrassing to have to explain to St. Peter that your cause of death was a falling coconut, but apparently he will have heard the story before. I suppose the image of the waves of the Pacific rolling onto a sandy beach of a Hawaiian island might not be a bad last impression before the one the coconut leaves. And, I guess, the only other positive thing to say about all of this is that the trip to Paradise won't be a long one as you were already there when the coconut struck!

We discovered one of the must-see attractions on the island of Maui is the Road to Hana. We had rented a Chrysler 300, which is big by anyone's standards, but on a relatively small island, it felt like I was steering a Nimitz class aircraft carrier around a swimming pool. The *Maui Information Guide* describes the road this way, "With approximately 600 curves and 54 bridges, the *Road to Hana* can bring you closer to heaven in more ways than one." Yep, it sounded like a challenge. The others had to leave early for home so, with Ed and Carol in the back seat, we headed off to Hana.

The authors of the Information Guide do not exaggerate! It's a fifty-two-mile journey that took us over three hours to complete! It has indeed more than six hundred turns, many of which are of the hairpin variety and more than fifty bridges wide enough for one car. I think they were made for narrow cars, not the USS *Abraham Lincoln*, but somehow we made it. One of the reasons it takes so long is because there are places to stop to admire the view and we did that. But I also had to keep checking back to make sure that Ed and Carol were still with us in the back seat and that they hadn't turned the colour of the foliage from the wild, twisting ride. The reward at the end of the journey is the opportunity to buy a T-shirt that proclaims, "I Survived the Road to Hana." But beware! It doesn't say you survived the road back.

Kauai has a special charm as it's quiet and serene and only about 10 percent is accessible by car. The Waimea Canyon is breathtaking with its reddish rock and deep creases carved by volcanic activity thousands of years ago, and there are hiking trails everywhere. We also visited the town of Hanalei. You may recall the lyrics from the song made famous by Peter, Paul, and Mary, *"Puff, the magic dragon lived by the sea, and frolicked in the autumn mist in a land called Honah Lee..."* We were told by the locals that Honah Lee is really Hanalei and that "Puff the Magic Dragon" is really *not* about smoking marijuana. Well, everyone is entitled to their opinion.

We also had the opportunity to listen to a local couple performing on the ukulele and slack key guitar. For those who are not in tune with music, so to speak, slack key means exactly what it says. One or more of the strings is detuned or slacked with the tuning key. And it sounded incredible! It was just so relaxing with the breeze blowing through the glassless openings of the building we were in, the birds chirping their own form of musical accompaniment, and with the Hawaiian music and stories of the history of Hawaii landing softly on our ears. It was a magical moment and one that I will always cherish.

As I look around at the group in the hotel room in Miami thinking about Hawaii, the term "satori" inexplicably comes to my mind. "Satori" is a Japanese Zen Buddhist term that has stuck with me and it's described by the Online Free Dictionary as the "state of sudden indescribable intuitive enlightenment." Maybe it's possible to achieve that in Hawaii, I thought to myself. With the warm air, the sound of the waves gently rolling in and out, the apparent contentment of the people, could this be the place to find satori?

But then I remembered sitting beside an obviously stressed local commuter on a jaunt to one of the other islands and trying to strike up a conversation. The airline stewardess had just demonstrated the seat belt instructions and finished by saying "Mahalo," which is "Thank you" in Hawaiian. The woman beside me muttered, "If I hear 'Mahalo' one more time, I think I'll throw up."

"It's a beautiful day, don't you think?" I said.

"Yes, and it would be even better if they would shut off that damn Hawaiian music!"

Well, maybe even paradise has its limitations.

19

AFTER HEARING ABOUT the woman who wasn't enamored with the Hawaiian lifestyle, Jim the Jokemaster is prompted to say, "Do you know that men are like tiles to most women? If they are laid properly the first time, they can be walked on for the next twenty years." The men smile and the women laugh at that one.

Conversation quickly turns to how we got started travelling together in the first place. We visited them in their homes and they visited us but, eventually, we all thought it might be time to try a vacation together to enjoy neutral ground. Various options were bandied about, and finally it was decided to try a short cruise. None of us had ever cruised before and some had barely been on a boat. This could be interesting! We continued talking about how it all came about.

"Evelyn was designated as the trip organizer," Brenda recalls, "since she had a lot of experience in sending amateur boxers around the world through her job. What was your title again?" Evelyn says, "I was the accountant/administrative assistant. I was originally labelled a bookkeeper, but they upgraded my title to accountant when they couldn't afford to give me a raise." Everyone laughs and we recall that ground rules were established up front. If someone wanted to do something that no one else wanted to do, that was completely up to them. We believed that this number of related people travelling together could end in catastrophe so the rules had to be set. "In fact," says Linda, "Evelyn gave us all a bag of quarters and told us that if we had a problem, to call someone who cares." Everyone nods with a knowing smile.

Brenda goes on to say that Evelyn became known as the "Problem Solver" because she points everyone in the right direction. "She found the travel agent we all use, she ensures that we have enough time between flights, and she confirms we are all staying together at the same hotel. She even decided the destination of our first trip together and proposed the length of time. When we run into a problem, either individually or as a group, she always manages to find a way out because of her experience she's had in dealing with other difficult people."

We all laugh at Brenda's Freudian slip by her use of the term "other" difficult people. Evelyn adds to this by telling us about one of the directors in her organization complaining bitterly about the high cost that the office (Evelyn) was paying for airfare. He decided to make his own arrangements and, on the day of the meeting, he called Evelyn at her office and asked, "Where's the hotel? I can't find it, and the taxi driver doesn't seem to know where it is either." Evelyn asked him if he had the information memo that had been sent to him containing the hotel address. He said that it was at home, but he had written down the address. So Evelyn asked him what city he was in. He said, "Saint John, New Brunswick." To that Evelyn replied, "Well, you had better get on another airplane, then, because as per the information you were provided, you are supposed to be in St. John's, Newfoundland." That was a different Canadian province altogether. Needless to say he didn't complain anymore, and if anyone in our group ever feels the urge to do so, we will grab our quarter and call someone who cares because, frankly, Evelyn says she has heard it all and really doesn't want to hear it again.

Evelyn had always wanted to try a cruise so she decided on a four-night trip leaving from Miami with destinations of some place called Coco Cay, Nassau's Paradise Island, and Key West, Florida. Just in case anyone proved prone to sea sickness, a short cruise might be the answer. She also wasn't sure she could keep the farmers on the ship any longer!

It was an auspicious debut to international travel for the six from the prairies. We had checked into a Holiday Inn downtown in Miami, and the other six members of our group were supposed to meet us there. As Linda elaborates on their part of the beginning of the journey, it's fun to think of the story behind the story. These were six new tourists who are used to life on the farm where things are serene, peaceful, and generally orderly. Their introduction to international travel was far from that.

"We understood that we were to catch a shuttle bus to the hotel when we landed in Miami. However, as we were waiting for the shuttle bus to arrive, a call came over the public address system for us. We were told that there had been a change of plans and that we would be going to a different hotel. They loaded the six of us into a gigantic coach big enough for about sixty people and off we went to the new hotel.

"When we arrived at a palatial hotel, something just didn't seem right. There were ornate carvings everywhere and it just seemed to be too good to be true. We have nothing against the Holiday Inn, but this didn't seem to be in the same class. The first two floors were parking, the second two were high-end stores, and, finally, we arrived at the front desk dragging our suitcases behind us. The clerk at the desk said they had no reservation for us so we told him we thought we were supposed to be going to the Holiday Inn. He said he would check, but in the meantime, they obviously wanted to get six tired, scruffy, travel-weary people and their luggage out of the lobby. The Super Bowl was on so they gave us coupons for drinks so we could go into the bar to watch the game. We had seen the fireworks from the air as we flew over but by this time we just wanted to get to our rooms."

Linda continued, "The clerk at our temporary palace was gracious enough to call the Holiday Inn. The person he reached said that he would check and be right back. He never came back on the line. Presumably, he was watching the Super Bowl as most other people in North America would be doing. So I called and asked for the Finlays. There was no answer (we had gone for dinner) so then I asked for ourselves. 'Oh, they haven't checked in yet.'

"Of course we hadn't! We were sitting in a palatial hotel where we didn't belong on the other side of town, also where we didn't belong. So, we all grabbed our luggage and trundled off to find a taxi. We found one downstairs, and the driver wasn't very happy as he was just finishing his fast food dinner. He grumbled that he would take us but that it would be impossible to fit every piece of luggage into his trunk. We said we would make it fit. We put what we could in the trunk and the rest sat on our laps. Now, instead of six of us on a sixty-passenger bus, there were seven of us, including the driver, scrunched together in a car with luggage on our laps!

"As we headed off, we started to notice bars on the windows of the houses and razor wire on some of the fences. We thought this can't be good. When the driver stopped at a light he put his wrappers and remnants of his meal on the boulevard. Someone started screaming at him, and we really expected the next thing we would see would be a muzzle flash and a bullet lodging itself somewhere too close to where we were sitting. The driver took off with tires squealing, and we proceeded down the freeway at over eighty miles per hour. Finally, after our tour of Miami, we arrived at our destination at the Holiday Inn, where we were supposed to be in the first place."

Evelyn and I were pleased to see them when they finally walked in. Our imaginations had been working overtime as we sat and watched the Super Bowl on television in the comfort of our room.

Linda adds that in all the times we have travelled together, she rarely gets the smoking room she requests. Hers and Ron's room always seems to be smaller than the rest as well. She has visited the desk clerk on many occasions shortly after seeing their room. It's a mystery. No one can dispute what she is saying and we move on.

We were in awe of the cruise ship when we arrived at the dock the next day. It was something like seeing a mountain superimposed on a dark blue sky for the first time. It was quite a shock seeing the ships glistening in the port with their stark white hulls in contrast with the blue water. Twelve storeys tall and two and a half football fields long, the power required to actually get these things to move is unimaginable. Stepping aboard is like arriving in another world; opulence doesn't begin

I GUESS WE MISSED THE BOAT

to describe this colossus of the seas. It's like stepping into a small city owned by an oil sheik. And a city it is, with every size, shape, nationality, and everything anyone could ever want within easy walking distance. It's our little piece of the world for the next few days, along with about three thousand of our closest friends.

There was little time to explore as the first order of business was the lifeboat drill. This was all news to us, but given recent events with the *Costa Concordia*, looking back we are happy that we had to go through that slightly annoying exercise. Evelyn had inadvertently caused some consternation among her sisters by giving them a copy of *The Poseidon Adventure* for Christmas soon after we had booked the cruise. I am sure it was done with the best of intentions and I am equally sure that everyone in our group was happy to know where the lifeboats were.

The lifeboat drill involved going to our designated spot, putting on our life vests, and standing there in the hot sun cracking inappropriate jokes about hoping the captain keeps the shiny side up. It sometimes takes a few minutes as there are always those who think they don't need to show up, being above the rules. Admittedly, at the time of this, our first cruise, it was difficult to imagine one of these things ever running aground, let alone sinking, unless it was hit by a giant tsunami or something. And if something happened, the captain would never abandon the ship until all of us were off safely, right? Unless, of course, he was accidentally bumped into a life raft in the chaos, as the passengers ran frantically around without any instruction and the ship listed dangerously to one side. No, THAT could never happen!

After the lifeboat drill, we got to explore the moveable castle where we would be staying for the next three days. The staterooms are small, but functional. With so many things to do, we weren't going to be spending much time in them anyway. The toilets, which Jim affectionately named "Slurpee," have tremendous suction, and you feel that you need to stand back when you flush them for fear of being sucked in and jettisoned into the ocean. As a male, I'm not sure it would be wise to remain sitting on the toilet when you flush as you might be neutered before you realized what was happening.

Everything is small in the room. To match everything else, the showers are also small. Our son talks about soaping the walls of the showers in some hotels he had stayed in so that he could move. The showers in the ship are something like that. But like any recreational vehicle, everything that one needs is in the room and everything has a place. Of course, there are bigger rooms for the well-heeled but the one we're in is a designer's dream and contributes significantly to the cruising experience . . . in a small way.

As we wandered around the ship, we found nine bars, a library, a spa, jogging track, fitness room, Internet area, mini-putt, theatre for live entertainment, cinema, etc. Apparently, there was even a morgue onboard, although we really didn't want to test that theory. There was food available all the time, and there were people lounging like beached whales until the time came to roll off their chaise and waddle into one of the multiple dining areas to replenish. I guessed they feared they wouldn't have enough calories stored to make it back to their deck chairs and survive until the urge to eat struck them again.

Once we were out in the sunshine and starting to explore the deck, Evelyn took it upon herself to get my brothers-in-law to remove their socks while wearing sandals. It took some convincing, and removal of the socks revealed shockingly white legs running from the bottom of the hem of the shorts to the end of the toes. I believe that was the last time socks and sandals made an appearance at the same time on the same feet!

After that, it was fun in the sun as we enjoyed the decadence that is cruising. We all met to go off on our first adventure in the Bahamas and, one by one, each member of the group pulled out their Tilley hat. Tilley hats are made in Canada and, according to their website, they should be considered one of the wonders of the modern world. They are guaranteed and insured for life, they float, they are waterproof, they have a secret pocket, they won't shrink, and there were six of them sitting jauntily upon six heads above six smirking faces. We decided to go with the group anyway, and, as we were walking down the beach, someone approached us, pointed to Evelyn and me, and said, "Well, it's obvious these two are the rookies in this group." Rookies, indeed! We invested in our own Tilleys when we got home.

The one great thing about everyone wearing the same hat is that, if for some reason you are separated from the group, it is just a matter of looking for the Tilleys so that you can join up again. I add that the WOBLIDIX T-shirts would have accomplished the same thing but get no response.

We had our first international experience in the straw market in Nassau. They were pretty insistent that we buy something. Of course, they are only trying to eke out a living and you can't blame them for trying. There was any number of vendors selling everything from straw hats to carvings. As I was walking down the dock through the vendors, a woman ran toward me with a baseball hat and put it on my head. She said $15. I said, "I don't want a hat," and tried to give it back. She said that it would be a real deal at $10 and put it back on my head. I said, "I don't want a hat," and gave it back. She said, "You can have it for $5," and put it back on my head. I once again, more forcefully, told her I didn't want it. She angrily whipped it off my head like it was entirely my fault for wasting her precious time and stomped after another potential customer. Where was Ed the Negotiator when I needed him? Oh, he was off negotiating something else, which Carol would be dutifully noting in her journal. Too bad! He would have acquired it for next to nothing if the vendor was willing to let it go for so little.

I did negotiate for a carving called a Bahama Mama that was a caricature of a native woman with exaggerated features. It was really heavy and the thought unfortunately occurred to me that it would seriously weigh down my suitcase, so even though I could have had it for a great price, I decided to leave it there. I made my way back to the ship and told Evelyn about the Bahama Mama and, as I did, I decided I really should have bought it. She said, "It's too late. The ship will be leaving in fifteen minutes." There was another lesson learned here. If you want something, get it while you have the chance.

While it seems unfair to haggle with people who don't have two cents to rub together, it is expected practice in the Caribbean. The vendor would rather make a sale than not, but they have limits and will not sell their goods when that limit is reached. If you are wearing expensive jewellery when negotiations take place, the starting price is going to be much higher. You can have fun when you haggle but don't think you will get it for nothing. The vendors are trying to make a living and deserve to make a reasonable return on their products. We found that enjoying the negotiation and treating the vendors with respect will allow us to walk away feeling that we have scored a great deal and they will be able to put food on their table for another day.

As it turned out, the mystery called Coco Cay is a small island owned by, and for the exclusive use of, the cruise line. It's a tiny island with the most beautiful white sand beaches you will ever see and water that is translucent. Most of our gang had never snorkeled before, and with the opportunity to walk out from the beach, this was the perfect chance. We all donned our snorkel gear and headed out. But before going, I learned one of those lessons about growing older that I really didn't want to have to learn.

I have developed a patch at the back of my head that is particularly barren. I prefer not to think about it. Out of sight, out of mind and all that. I have now come to the point where if someone tells me my hair is thinning, I am delighted because it means I still have some!

We were all lathering up with suntan lotion in anticipation of heading out into the sparkling ocean. Since we weren't far removed from winter climes and our bodies were nearly as white as the glistening sand we were standing on, it was a necessity. In fact, I wondered if people would look in our direction and only see bathing suits as our bodies blended in with the sand. As we lathered up, sister-in-law and medical practitioner Brenda came over and plopped some lotion on the back of my head. "What are you doing?" I yelped. I hate the feel of lotion anywhere on me but to have it mixed in with the hair surrounding the shiny spot was particularly offensive. However, she explained how that spot would attract the sun's rays like flies to a candle, so into the water I went with my bald spot glistening with suntan lotion.

Snorkeling at Coco Cay is like being in another world. There are wrecks placed in the water that you can swim down to along with the multicoloured fish that appear and disappear in and out of the various holes in the wrecks. It is easy to lose track of time as you drift in the beautifully warm water. In fact, Evelyn did lose track of time. We wondered if she was swimming back to Miami, but eventually she emerged from the water, tired and completely satisfied that she had made the right decision to get us all on a cruise.

There are many things to do on the ship to stay occupied while at sea. There are the many bars, of course. There are pools to lie around with the strains of calypso music beating in the background. You can watch the most redneck of sports, the belly flop competition, and if you have been in training for some time and have the twenty-four-pack abs to qualify, you can even participate! People can just lounge on the deck chairs or the health nuts on the ship can walk around the deck. Four times around represents a mile. Or there is mini-putt. The brothers-in-law and I decided to try mini-putt on the cruise. It's a nice layout near the back of the ship so, as we were putting, the blue sea formed a backdrop for the green surface of the mini-putt course and the colourful golf balls.

The Cowboy was lining up his first putt, and the ship lurched a little just as he was taking his shot. The ball rocketed toward the hole, then past and over the edge of the mini-putt surface. Once it hit the concrete deck it picked up speed. There was the little red ball bouncing along past unsuspecting passengers on its way to the stairwell and the next deck below. We watched as it bounded down each step, each bounce a little higher than the last until it landed unceremoniously on Deck 11. It went unimpeded along its merry way until it finally came to rest under a deck chair bearing a rather large passenger. Undeterred by this minor inconvenience, Cowboy Ron trotted down the stairs after the ball, said, "Excuse me" to the large gentleman in the chair, reached underneath him to grab the golf ball, and we continued the game.

After sailing the open seas for a while, the next port of call was Key West in the Florida Keys. We took a tour along the sun-drenched, palm-lined streets, observing the houses that could have been constructed from ginger bread. It's like stepping back into the Victorian era as we pass massive mansions, rich in tradition with former owners like Ernest Hemingway and the thirty-third U.S. president, Harry S. Truman.

Almost everyone on the bus got to see all of this rich history with both eyes. Brenda, on the other hand, chose to videotape the entire tour so she was observing everything through a one-inch-square lens. I don't know to this day if she has seen Key West or if she has been able to remove the mark of the lens from around her eye where it was firmly planted for an hour and a half.

That was the end of our first cruise and everyone was thoroughly pleased with the experience. There would undoubtedly be more. But the picture of Brenda with the impression of the camera lens around her eye is too good to pass up. Cruise stories will have to be put on hold for the moment. It's time to talk about video camera antics.

20

VIDEO CAMERAS have evolved considerably over the years. In fact, it would have been nice if we'd had one to capture the whales breaching in Hawaii . . . but we didn't. Of course, we no longer have to lug around twenty-pound cameras and fool around with tapes. Life in the camera world is much simpler now, but it's the video that comes out that is particularly interesting.

But does anyone watch a video they have taken more than once, if at all? Maybe for comic relief! The video camera has provided a good deal of that. We had the good fortune to be at Cape Kennedy for the launch of a rocket that would ultimately fly through the tail of a comet many years later. We were all jammed into a tower, miles away from the launch, and we had no idea what direction we were supposed to be looking. Someone headed for one side of the tower so we all dutifully followed, like sheep following Little Bo Peep. There was no chance of these sheep losing their way. We were all keeping Bo Peep firmly in view. Brenda is, at five feet tall, slightly vertically challenged and she managed to become the de facto white-haired, fanny-pack-carrying Bo Peep as she moved to the front of the mass of humanity so she could train her camera in the direction everyone was looking. She and her ever-present fanny pack disappeared as she wound her way in among the crowd of faithful rocket watchers.

The countdown could be heard over the loud speakers. There was much anticipation in the tower as we waited. I was an ardent follower of the space program while I was growing up so this was a special day for me. ". . . 5-4-3-2-1 Lift Off! We have lift-off, ladies and gentlemen." There was the brilliant white rocket lifting off the launch pad in a fiery display of immense power with giant plumes of smoke billowing out from all sides superimposed over the clear azure sky. But we didn't see it. *We were on the wrong side of the freakin' tower!*

We all rushed to the other side of the tower and Brenda inadvertently left her video camera on. Since she was at the front of the pack for the expected launch, she was at the back going to the other side and she filmed a bunch of rear ends racing ahead of her. We did decide to watch the video once, and there was the clear blue Florida sky, followed by a thundering herd of bums, and then the vapor trails of the rocket, which, by this time, was well on its way to chasing the comet it would ultimately catch some ten years later.

I'm not sure what it is with the fascination for filming butts around our place. While I laughed uproariously at Brenda's misfortunes with the camera, I had my own experience with "leaving-the-camera-turned-on-at-the-worst-possible-moment" syndrome. As I relate the story to the group, I can see Brenda is the most relieved at not being the only one to have left the switch on at the most inopportune time.

Evelyn and I were on the Capilano Suspension Bridge, one of Vancouver's best attractions. It's 450 feet across and hangs 230 feet above the raging Capilano River. Even though it's firmly attached to some giant Douglas fir trees, the bridge still sways and the thought occurs that it could break at any moment as people make their way, bouncing, across the bridge. But it's an impressive sight to see and well worth the visit. It seems like a long way across, and I had to keep one hand on the cable at the side as I walked. Evelyn wasn't too keen about going at all.

I had the trusty video camera in my other hand as we made our way across. But once again, the on-off switch managed to find its way to the "on" position as we bounced across. A subsequent viewing by the family alternated between the slats of the bridge and Evelyn's butt for half of the journey. Eventually, I realized that the camera was on when we were about half way across and started filming the view that we had actually paid to see.

The view on the other side of the bridge is incredible, and it is possible to walk along through the treetops via a boardwalk.

And sometime we will learn to operate the camera properly or at least edit the film before showing it to the family, though it would not be nearly as entertaining!

There was more. When we were in Cuba, our eldest son made me promise to bring him a photo of a topless bather; so, not wanting to disappoint, I surreptitiously tried to photograph one or two of the firmer ones while aiming my camera at an unsuspecting palm tree. It wasn't working out too well. I couldn't blatantly take a picture of a sleeping sunbather without feeling some guilt. I mean, come on! My mother, who was worried about the divorce from the trip to Wyoming, would have been mortified. So I did the best I could and got many photos of palm trees and ocean but none that were decipherable enough for our son. I would have to describe the pictures to him in detail.

However, Evelyn unknowingly did it for me. We had a new movie camera with us, and she decided to shoot some footage of me while I was "frolicking" in the surf. I swam, I dove, and I floated on my back. I came, I saw, I conquered the surf. We had not previewed the footage and when we showed it to our sons and their respective girlfriends, there I was cavorting in the water. But just off to the side was an indescribable beauty emerging from the water topless in Bo Derek style! (For those who may not remember, Bo Derek came to prominence in the movie *"10"* in 1979. A poster of her in a bathing suit emerging from the water adorned the walls of many young males in the early eighties.) My wife was so focused on capturing me in the water, she was completely oblivious to the young lady beside me. While I may have failed with the photos, Evelyn more than made up for it with the video, and there were gales of laughter and merciless teasing from the audience.

We realized that we had been momentarily sidetracked from talking about the cruise by our escapades with the video camera. There was one incident following our first cruise when I would have liked to have had a video camera. After disembarking, we had made our way to the airport where we were once again waiting for our respective flights. My three one-syllable in-laws, Ron, Jim, Ed, and I were walking through the airport when a gentleman from somewhere else in full ceremonial dress came walking toward us.

Not everyone realizes this, but there are some people who are just incapable of whispering, and Cowboy Ron is one of those. I guess he had never seen someone dressed like the person coming toward us. The gentleman was tall and good looking and he wore a coat of many, many, many colours, which I am sure would have been the envy of any man in his culture. However, it was just too much for Ron. "JEEEZUS, WOULD YOU GET A LOAD OF THAT GUY!" We quickly veered off before a ceremonial weapon emerged from the ceremonial costume to slice us into ceremonial bits.

By contrast, Ron, being the cowboy that he is, was wearing his blue jeans with a belt buckle about the size of the one presented to the World Wrestling Federation champion and a shirt with more silver buttons than you could count running up and down the sleeves. Ron would have been the envy of any cowboy in North America! I'm sure we would have heard the gentleman coming toward us exclaiming something similar about Ron as we approached, but he could probably whisper!

It really is fun to travel with these people. We're never quite sure what's going to happen next. If nothing else, we share a lot of laughs.

21

WE HAD DECIDED as a group we liked cruising so much that we would lengthen the voyage the next time. In a strictly democratic fashion, we voted and chose a five-night western Caribbean cruise with stops in Jamaica and Grand Cayman. There were ten of us travelling together this time as some friends, Randy and Nadine, who weren't related to anyone among us, were brave enough to join us.

As I mentioned earlier, Linda is a nurse and is required to work shift work. As all shift workers will tell you, it's sometimes difficult to get to sleep when the opportunity presents itself, so rather than sleeping before their flight to Florida where we would board the ship, she decided to watch a movie. Linda says, "Before leaving on this cruise, I saw *My Big Fat Greek Wedding*. I managed to come into the movie after it had started, and it seemed to be pretty good . . . the first time. Unfortunately, the same movie was playing on the airplane on the way to Miami." At that time, there was no choice of movie; it was that or nothing. Everyone among us remembers that we were stuck watching that movie or sleeping.

There are also movie theatres on the ship and they were proudly announcing that this fantastic movie would be playing. "Again I was having trouble sleeping so I went into the theatre to see what the movie was. It was *My Big Fat Greek Wedding* and it was in exactly the same spot as it was when I saw it at home!" When we were on the airplane to fly home and were in the air, the stewardess announced the name of the movie that would be showing. "I couldn't believe it," says Linda. "It was *My Big Fat Greek Wedding*." We all laugh as we did on the plane that day. Well, most of us. Nine passengers nearly fell out of their seats laughing, 173 wondered what the fuss was about, and one threw her hands up in the air and rolled her eyes. The nine passengers ruled the day as the stewardess thankfully figured out that the movie was not the most popular choice and switched it to something that, fortunately, Linda hadn't seen. Who said the passenger doesn't come first? Linda finishes her story by proclaiming, "Man, I hate that movie!!"

We were once again placed in a decent hotel in downtown Miami, about an hour from the cruise ship terminal. We were all excited the morning of departure and we waited patiently for the shuttle bus that was to take us to our ship. Everyone was laughing, completely relaxed and dressed in our finest warm weather clothing, even though the locals were parading around outside in parkas, mitts, and earmuffs. That's the difference between coming from Canada to a warm climate in the middle of winter and being born and raised in one.

We waited patiently in the comfort of the hotel lobby as the minutes ticked by. The minutes turned to tens of minutes, and our travel arranger, Evelyn the Problem Solver, started to make phone calls. As the rest of us kept vigil, she was told that the shuttle bus would be arriving imminently. One or two approached, raising our hopes, only to dash them again as they drove on by. She called again and was told the same thing. As yet another bus drove by, tempting us like a breast of chicken under the nose of a starving man, Evelyn called a third time. They had forgotten us!

The comfort of the hotel suddenly evaporated as vitriol rained down from the stranded group. We turned from a joyful, fun-loving group full of anticipation, into a snarling, heaving pack of wolves, focused on its prey. It was difficult to clearly identify exactly who or what that prey was as it could have been the travel agent, the tour company, the hotel, the shuttle bus company ... All that was really apparent was that someone was going to have to pay. With teeth gnashing, there were howls of, "Why did they book us here?" "How could they forget us?" "I'll never travel with them again!" Of course, none of this venting would do us any good at this stage, but it was a relief to blow off steam.

I GUESS WE MISSED THE BOAT

There was nothing we could do but wait for the bus to show up, and Evelyn carried out her problem-solving duties by keeping the phone line open until the bus actually did arrive. Only one problem remained. The driver had to get us to our destination on time. We were barely strapped into our seats when the front wheels of the bus squealed as it launched into the wild ride to come. Carol didn't even take out her notebook for this ride! We dashed through the streets of Miami, like the fabled Greyhounds at the track hot on the tail of the mechanical rabbit. The Greyhound would never catch that rabbit, but will earn a treat like doggie biscuits or something for crossing the finish line; our reward would be a ride on a big shiny boat . . . if we lived to see it.

We careened around the final corner and headed into the terminal area, and the collective sigh of relief in the shuttle was palpable. That snarling pack of wolves returned to being a purring group of pussycats. I am not sure if it was the sight of the big ship or the fact that the group's concentration had been intensely focused on their white knuckles burrowing tiny trenches in the nearest handholds that caused the unnerving quiet in the van. The fact that the ship was still there was a great relief.

There's some benefit to being the last ones to arrive. No lineups! We made it through check-in in record time and over the gangplank just as they were about to lift it. But Linda reminds us that they were not as fortunate. They were held up over their paperwork. Linda says, "As we ran for the gangplank, it was starting to rise. I said to Ron, 'I guess we missed the boat.' As you know, he can't whisper anyway so he was yelling that we were coming. We ran up and explained that the rest of our group was all on board and they lowered the gangplank again. They were not very happy. I told them that we and a lot of other people who just got on the ship ahead of us weren't very happy either!"

There's another downside to being late. We missed the lifeboat drill. Most of us had been through it before, but Randy and Nadine were new to this cruising thing. The problem was compounded by Nadine's tendency toward motion sickness. The race through Miami, coupled with the anticipation of getting on a ship that, well, moves, raised her anxiety level. They wanted to be part of the lifeboat drill to help relieve the stress, but it was not to be. No drill for us on this trip.

It got worse.

Earlier, we remarked on the sheer immensity of these giants of the seas. This particular one had twelve decks, was 880 feet long, and weighed in at over 73,000 tonnes! You would expect it to move through the water with ease, cutting through waves of any size without budging, controlling and patrolling the seas as if it owned them. But consider this. The 2004 tsunami in Sri Lanka knocked a train off its tracks and deposited it in some trees! The power of the seas is even greater than the giants that patrol them. If it's a battle between water and anything, anything is going to lose!

Sitting at dinner, it's possible to look out the window and watch the horizon go up and down, up and down. At least that is what the mind wants you to believe. But it isn't the horizon that's moving, of course. It's this massive ship that is being buffeted by the waves. It's not unpleasant and one quickly gets used to it, but when you have motion sickness, the chances of taking on a shade of colouring like Kermit the Frog are unpleasantly enhanced.

It got worse still.

As we were walking toward the live theatre that night, we were noticeably bouncing back and forth off the walls. The waves were getting stronger. It was not only the live entertainment that was rocking and rolling. So were we! After the show, the other guys and I went a different direction than the girls and somehow we ended up at a pool table in one of the bars. Now, imagine trying to play pool with the ship going up and down and the balls rolling around on the table. A waiter came along and said rather sarcastically, "Having a little trouble, boys?" Jim said equally sarcastically, "Only what you would notice." The waiter reached under the table and made an adjustment and the tabletop magically started moving in unison with the ship. There was a gyroscope on the tabletop that evened out its movement. Man, these ship designers are good!

Of course, *we* were still moving up and down as we tried to shoot so it was still impossible to play. I have no idea why we decided to play pool that night. I certainly know why the table was free. Nobody in their right mind wanted to play!

The waves got higher throughout the night; at one point, the water was coming up to our window, and we were on the fourth floor! We felt for Nadine that night, and she did, in fact, have a complexion like Kermit, at least colour-wise, the next morning. However, everyone survived the night, although I'm sure a few of the passengers left a little of their dinner behind.

We learned that it's much more fun cruising with people you know. Passengers are assigned seats at dinner and if you are not compatible with your meal companions, it could be a chore. You can always complain to your headwaiter and ask to be moved, but that's not really something you want to have to do.

Travelling together as a group makes things simple. We

usually find one, if not all, of the group for breakfast and lunch and we always sit together for dinner. But sometimes at breakfast and lunch, we don't find our gang and we end up sitting with others. Evelyn and I sat with a group one day for lunch and it was an indication of what things could be like.

First there were the young newlyweds. Things were not happy in new marriage land for some reason, and they were bickering at the table. She was clearly unhappy about something he had done. Didn't she realize that there would be plenty of opportunities to be mad at him for things he did or didn't do or allegedly did or didn't do later in their married life? Uncomfortable!

To their left was a couple who didn't speak English and made no effort to. Obviously, on an international cruise that will happen. No problem there. However, even when the lady of the twosome made an observation in her native language, he responded with a grunt and kept eating. Finally, there was the couple who described this ship as the lowest class of transportation that they had ever been unfortunate enough to travel on. Nothing was good enough . . . the accommodation, the food, the service, the excursions, the staff . . . everything was beneath them. It would clearly be the last time they ever travelled with that particular cruise line. At least, we hoped so, for fear of ever having the misfortune of being anywhere near them in the future.

As our group sits around the dinner table on a cruise, the subject can turn to pretty much anything. But there is a ritual that occurs before each meal. Evelyn and I didn't actually get to participate in this ritual for the first few years until we earned the right. That gave us the opportunity to sit back, observe, and learn. Like rookies at a professional training camp, we were in a position to gain valuable experience by being on the front line, watching the veterans.

The ritual begins with everyone delving into pockets and purses, searching around for something that is obviously extremely valuable. The value can be measured by the look of consternation on the faces of those who have merely misplaced it to the look of panic on those who are coming to the realization that they may have actually lost it. Most nights everyone is able to locate the article and the ritual continues. It's a container they are looking for and, once it's located, it's placed carefully on the table. The containers vary in size and complexity, but it's not the container itself that is important. No, the container is only plastic, but it has a number of compartments. The real object of the ritual is located inside the compartments, and, often, each compartment holds many of them.

While this ritual is practised individually and no one waits for the other to have located their object of desire, it's almost a team sport as the objects appear on the table at virtually the same time. In my mind's eye, I can see the symphony playing in the background. With the imagined strains of *Swan Lake* and the soft lighting from the giant chandeliers overhead providing the ambience, it is like watching a synchronized swimming event. Arms looping in synchronization toward pocket or purse. Fingers searching. Discovery. Containers placed on the table at precisely the same time. Compartments opened simultaneously.

Opening the container brings about a look on the faces of the participants in this ritual like the face of Gollum upon seeing the shiny ring in the *Lord of the Rings*. "My Precious!!"

But even though the container has many compartments, the participants in the ritual restrain themselves and open only one. Because today is Tuesday. And specific pills have to be taken on Tuesday. Yes, we are all "of an age" that sadly brings about certain changes in our health. So everyone has their pill containers that control things like blood pressure, cholesterol, stomach ailments, hearts that are pumping too fast, hearts that are pumping too slow, prostates the size of grapefruits, bladders that hamsters would be proud of, and the list goes on.

I almost felt left out on the first few trips watching the others with their precious pill containers, but alas, Evelyn and I eventually joined the club and participate in the ritual along with the rest. We all have to pay for the privilege of being older, and this, unfortunately, is one of the payments we are obliged to make. We're all now in training for the day Synchronized Pill Popping becomes an Olympic event. As the world's population ages, I don't think it can be far off.

Our first stop was Labadee in Haiti. It is not difficult to see that Haiti is the poorest of the poor as we were taken on a walking tour of the town and outskirts of Labadee. This was long before the devastation of the earthquake. They're fortunate that the cruise ships stop there as it has to do something for the economy.

As we walked, we stopped to rest at one point about half way through the tour. There were a number of us on the walking tour and we eventually made our way back to the town. It was time to take more pictures but there was something missing. My camera! I remembered setting it down when we stopped at the rest stop, which happened to be as far away as it could possibly be. I did the only thing I could. I ran back to where I had left it. As I ran up to the spot where I knew it had been, my heart that was pounding away by this time was rudely interrupted as it did a free fall in my chest. The camera wasn't there! Fortunately, there were not many photos on it. I had taken one of Linda on a floating mat with the cruise ship in the background that might have been awesome.

The spot where the camera had been was again a simple rock with nothing manmade embellishing it. The camera could have been picked up by a local but it could have just as easily been picked up by someone from the cruise who was on the same tour as we were. We mentioned it to the local police who were not particularly helpful, and finally it was time to go back to the ship. It could have been worse. It could have been my passport. It could have been my pass to get on the ship. It could have been the person who stole my camera who went missing. Now *that* would have been karma! But alas it was not to be, and it bothered me that I had been stupid enough to leave it unprotected in plain sight.

Back on board, I told the pursers at the desk that I had lost my camera. They looked in Lost and Found and determined that in this case the lost was still lost and the found was not

I GUESS WE MISSED THE BOAT

what I was looking for. So, I did the only thing that was left to do. I called my insurance company.

"One moment, please," said the clerk who answered. "Wait a min—" I said as she disappeared. I'm *waiting* on a ship to shore phone. Do you know what they charge by the minute on a ship to shore phone? Well, neither did I . . . until I got the bill. It was $80 to put in my claim!!

As I relate this story to the group, I am reminded of my second trip to Tanzania. Since Evelyn and I were going back to see the results of some fundraising we had been doing, I wanted to maintain my blog back home. I had a smart phone so when I could get a signal, I would enter some information into my blog and I uploaded a couple of photos. It worked well, and I was very happy to be able to maintain the blog so that interested people could follow what we were doing. But my phone wasn't smart enough to tell me I was being stupid.

I knew I was roaming but I thought that the number of entries I was making would not amount to much. We were home for about a month and all the travel expenses had been paid. Then my cellular phone bill came in. It was $350!! I couldn't believe it. My fellow travellers in the room (who are not counted among the technologically savvy) just about passed out. I explained how I called my service provider to complain about the bill, and after practically crying on the phone, they decided that since I was a first time offender they would cut the bill in half. I was somewhat relieved and made an oath to myself that I would never roam again. I am tempted to make a joke about giving me a home where the buffalo roam but I decide that jokes are Jim's domain and let it go.

But my nightmare wasn't over. Unbeknownst to me, that was only half the bill. The rest of the bill came in the following month. It was another $350!! I was back on the phone again, complaining about the high cost of roaming,, and they were good enough to cut it in half again since it was simply part of the same trip. It still cost $350 for a few updates to my blog! I sure hope my blog readers appreciated what they read!!

Our next stop was Jamaica; the ship managed to pull into its designated port, and the shore excursions were undertaken with no problem. We landed at the village of Ocho Rios, and, as with all Caribbean islands that we visited, it is vibrant and beautiful. Apparently, Ocho Rios means Eight Rivers in Spanish, but there is no sign of eight rivers in the area that we could see. The village of Ocho Rios is alive with people . . . and blaring horns! This is *not* like the corner of West 50th and 11th Avenue in New York where there is a sign that says "Don't Honk. $350 Fine." No, drivers here have one hand on the wheel and the other on the horn as they vie for space in this picturesque community on the oceanfront. It's a cacophony of sound as the horns blare for every apparent and often no apparent reason. If you are looking for a quiet, sedate place for a vacation, downtown Ocho Rios isn't it.

One of the highlights of the area is the multi-tiered rainforest shower known as Dunn's River Falls. It's about six hundred feet of water dropping down from one terrace to the next and onward in its inexorable march to the beach below. Tourists are allowed to climb up the falls, hand-in-hand with their fellow travellers and with the aid of a guide. It's a refreshing adventure, although the rocks are a little slippery as you make your way up. It takes about an hour and a half, including stops for pictures along the way. The group is encouraged to stop a few times, preferably lying back against the rocks with the water cascading down over us in a typical touristy pose for the professional photos that they will happily sell us.

At the top is a special surprise. When we were there, it was impossible to get away from the falls unless we exited through a craft market. It was dark and dingy with the sunshine blocked by the many trees that line the corridor of shops. It was absolutely full of Jamaican artisans who were all anxious to coax us into their even darker shops. They were aggressive in their pursuit of business; they all seemed about eight feet tall with braided hair and deep voices and they didn't want us to leave without purchasing something. If we made eye contact, we were instantly the next in line to be aggressively approached to buy a craft. If we didn't make eye contact, we could feel hostile looks at our backs as we made our way along the row. There were shouts of, "Over here" as we walked along as quickly as possible. While we have visited many other craft markets, we had not seen anything quite like this.

It could well have changed since then, as I am sure the approach was not particularly successful. I can't imagine many people enjoy being browbeaten into buying crafts. We told our fellow travellers that we would highly recommend the Dunn's River Falls attraction but to be prepared for hyper aggressive selling at the top. I read recently that the craft sellers feel that they're being forced out of business. Attraction operators are recommending that tourists do not buy anything directly from the artisans. Perhaps there is a reason why they were so aggressive. On the other hand, perhaps a business model involving aggressive sales tactics does not promote happy tourism. It got to the point of being scary, and we were relieved to finally find an exit with one or two craftsmen hot on our heels.

We carried on with the cruise to our next stop at Grand Cayman. While watching the world go by on the ship, we were given a special surprise of free drinks for a two-hour span. We all took advantage of it but none more than Ed the Negotiator. He managed to negotiate his share and a few more. What a guy! We were standing around chatting, and one of the individuals we were chatting to showed us his cast. He had rented a scooter for his excursion in Jamaica and apparently didn't hear the car horn. Or maybe he heard a hundred horns at the same time and didn't pay much attention. Somehow he managed to pile up the scooter and received a broken wrist for his troubles. He had the break set at the local clinic and we couldn't believe our eyes. His hand was at an odd angle from his arm. The medical practitioners among us, Brenda and Linda, cheered him up by telling him it would have to be broken again and reset by a doctor when he got home.

Once again the seas were rough, and those of us who had excursions planned were invited into the lounge area before leaving on our money-burning adventure. There the cruise team advised us that some of the excursions were cancelled due to high winds. We would not be swimming with the stingrays on this day! The ship was unable to dock so anyone going ashore would have to do so by tender. That isn't really a problem if you don't mind bobbing around like a cork and jostling your friends on a small boat as it rises and falls on the trip to shore.

Since the stingrays would sadly be swimming without us, the women had time to shop and the boys and I found a nice bar overlooking the bay. My impression is that Grand Cayman is a lot like other Caribbean islands, only more expensive. Clearly it would have been possible to pick up a nice real Rolex or some diamond earrings on the credit card. Unfortunately, the banks seem to like to be paid when you do that. So we declined, with thanks!

We bobbed back to the boat on the tender, and it nestled up against the gangplank that led to the safety of the big mother ship. Getting on the gangplank was going to be tricky. The tender was bobbing and the mother ship was bobbing but, due to the size discrepancy, they weren't exactly bobbing in unison. Gaps kept appearing between the gangplank and the tender so it was necessary to time the leap onto the gangplank when the bob of the tender and the bob of the ship were relatively even. Unfortunately, one woman didn't; her foot caught and she suffered a severe crack, sprain, or break. Good thing there is a sick bay on the ship and better to be repaired there than in the local hospital as evidenced with the right-angle wrist we saw earlier!

After this incident, the ship's captain decided to turn the ship around so that people would board from their tenders on the leeward side (or something). Anyone who was expecting to come back from Grand Cayman immediately were in for a wait as it took more than forty acres to turn this crate around. Eventually, they got it around and people were able to board with Rolexes and diamonds in hand.

On holidays, you'd expect that everyone will relax. But as we recall the disgruntled couple on the bus tour who lost their luggage, it's not necessarily the case. The Super Bowl has woven itself into a few of our adventures, and it happened again while

I GUESS WE MISSED THE BOAT

we were at sea. Randy and I decided to find a bar and watch part of the game on television. Of course, we all know that football is a religion for some and especially in the United States. While we Canadians worship at the Church of Hockey Night in Canada, Americans go to the Church of Monday Night Football. We understand that.

We got to the bar in plenty of time and found two seats with a clear view of the television set. The game started and Big Dude walked up and stood right in front of us. "Uh, excuse us. Would you mind moving over so we can see?" Big Dude lipped us off. "We were sitting here first. Could you find another spot?" Big Dude lipped us off some more. We lipped Big Dude back. Now remember, we are all on holidays on a luxurious cruise ship in the middle of the ocean on a beautifully warm night with nothing but sandy beaches and sunshine ahead of us for the next ten days. And we are about to get into a fight!?? I haven't been in a fight since Grade 6!!

Big Dude was tense and getting tenser. The veins were popping on his rather large neck as he curled and uncurled his ham-like hands. Things were escalating quickly. Finally, a kind older couple who could see what was happening scrunched over so that we could sit beside them and have a mostly unobstructed view again, even though the four of us were all a little uncomfortable in the spot that was meant for two. We were able to watch the game, and Big Dude and his buddies were left watching from their observation post in the middle of the floor, ensuring that no one could see around them.

Of course, we saw Big Dude and his loutish companions everywhere on the ship after that, but I don't think he even recognized us. Perhaps the sweetest moment came on the mini-putt course. My in-laws, Randy, and I were in a struggle for mini-putt domination with some of our American fellow travellers in a last man standing contest. It was intense competition and it came down to a head-to-head, winner-take-all tiebreaker between Randy and his American counterpart. Randy sank his putt. His competitor didn't. We prevailed, and I am sure it was quite devastating for the Americans to lose to some Canucks;

but in the postgame interview, we graciously pointed out that we won because we focused on one game at a time, overcame adversity, and played 110 percent.

Okay, maybe there was no postgame interview, but I should mention that the person who didn't sink his putt was none other than Big Dude! It was kind of fun watching his face redden as the blood rushed into it following his devastating loss. For him, the incident in the bar seemed to be a routine, brutish thing to do. I am not sure where someone like that ever relaxes if he can't do it on a cruise ship. It was all just a little sad.

Everyone gets what they deserve somewhere along the way. For us, it was a little redemption and we received medals that we proudly wore to the bar for our five o'clock drink. Can life get any sweeter?

22

WE NEXT LAUNCH into a discussion of the cost of travel and everyone agrees it's money well spent. Carol reaches for her notepad but no one is particularly interested in discussing the details. There is something about actually seeing some of the wonders of the world and meeting people from other cultures. Social networking and television certainly help us to know our fellow man, but it becomes even more apparent through travel that we are all the same with similar dreams and aspirations. Travel provides an excellent education. Some of us are fortunate enough to be born in a privileged part of the world, but everyone everywhere just wants peace and a little prosperity. Well, except for our illustrious leaders who seem to think we should have anything that belongs to somebody else. Jim suggests that government officials should have two terms; one to govern and the second in prison.

There is no doubt that getting to see all of this is expensive. But as Ron logically notes, "Once the money is spent, it's spent. Nothing will bring it back, and, hopefully, we can pay off the credit cards when we get home." Brenda says, "Oh, you mean the credit cards we use to pay off the onboard ship cards?" That puts a damper on the conversation as we all ponder those onboard ship cards.

I can't speak for all cruise lines, but the one we travel with uses a cashless system so we are each given cards that become our source of money for the duration of the cruise. Of course, the "cashless" cards have to be guaranteed by a credit card. But one tends to forget that, as travellers are tempted everywhere they go on the ship. You want a drink, sir? No problem. You would like to buy some nice jewellery for your wife or girlfriend? (Hopefully, they both have the same taste in case one notices a purchase that was intended for the other . . . but I digress.) Right this way! You want to take every excursion available on this trip and known to mankind? Step right up!

The shock is when the purser slides the bill under your door on the last day of the cruise. The first time or two on a ship it's highly recommended to have a defibrillator nearby when opening the envelope. While Carol may know how much was spent at any given moment on any given day from the detailed notes she has taken, most people don't worry about it until the bill comes. It's kind of kept track of mentally. And then it is OMG! From the rooms of first-time travellers all the way down the hall can be heard shouts of, "Clear!" as, one by one, the designated envelope opener is brought back to life by the onboard paramedics. Unfortunately, as the passengers awaken from their near death experiences, they slowly come to the awful realization that they still have that bill to pay.

As a group, we defied the near death experience and took another cruise; this time to the Panama Canal. It was pretty uneventful. We were placed in a hotel that was close to the port so we didn't have to race through town at breakneck speed to make our departure. We spent quite a bit of time at sea, but it was under the Caribbean sunshine. We had time to explore the ship, to lose a little money in the casino, to spend time on the deck lounges, and to play mini-putt. It was pretty relaxing.

The staff on cruise ships comes from every corner of the globe, and it is great to have the time to learn more about them and their culture. The staff enjoys passengers who are friendly and having a good time. They will laugh along with you and help make the experience just that much more enjoyable. They work long hours and some rely only on the tips they make. Often, they send their money home to their families. But in the end, we are all the same. It is a learning experience to hear of other cultures, and we all become richer as a result.

The first stop was Aruba. Being a landlubber, I was challenged to figure out exactly where we were on the water. Anyone who has driven with me will tell you it's not only on the water where I am directionally challenged. I rely on the captain of the ship to program the computer correctly or, if worse comes to worst, consult a map. As a last resort, if the captain is male, he could probably consult one of the women on the ship for directions, if he can stand to admit he has a problem!

After consulting the map, we determined that Aruba is a tiny island not far from the coast of Venezuela, and on a clear day, it's possible to see the coastline. It's actually the farthest away from home we will be on this trip. With its pristine beaches and colourful cookie-cutter houses, Aruba is yet another idyllic location nestled in the Caribbean Sea. Our first stop is a butterfly farm where we are able to see nature at its finest. Stepping into a tropical garden, there are butterflies of all shapes and sizes everywhere. Some are tiny, some are enormous, but they are all a reminder of nature's beauty. One landed on Jim the Jokemaster's hat, which prompted him to say, "Do you know how to make a butterfly? Shoot it out of the dish with your butter knife." I am sure this was not a rerun, because surely he wouldn't have the gall to tell it more than once, but it still drew groans from everyone who heard it.

Then it was on to see the world's longest natural bridge. Carved out of centuries of pounding surf, it was made of coral and would have been incredible to see . . . if it hadn't collapsed in 2005. Apparently, at one time it spanned over one hundred feet, but the sea built it and the sea exercised its option to take it away again. It collapsed on September 2 and *USA Today* quoted Tourism Minister Edison Briesen as saying, "It's a very sad day for Aruba and for its tourism. A picture of the bridge appears in almost every promotional flyer, and more tourists visit it than any other attraction."

Even though it had collapsed, we were taken to the site and tried to imagine what Mother Nature's carving would have been like before she decided to destroy her handiwork like some petulant two-year-old. I think we all felt a little twinge of sadness at not having come to this spot earlier to see what once was.

At night our group piled onto a catamaran for a sunset cruise. We motored out to sea with the wind blowing in our hair, the salt water on our faces, the setting sun burning the horizon above the water. The sun's rays were extended in a reflection across the sea like the strands of Rapunzel's hair. Those of you who have sailed know that once under sail, there is that incredible and uncanny calmness as the wind lightly buffets the sails above your head and the only other sound is the hiss of the waves lapping against the side of the boat.

The catamaran was cutting a clean swath through the water, leaving a white wake trailing along behind. But the quiet of sailing had been interrupted. By the time we reached the farthest point of our destination and the motors were shut down for the sail back home, large quantities of rum had been consumed and we expected Captain Jack Sparrow to emerge from the hold. The catamaran was rocking. Calypso music was blaring, and people were wobbling between the bar and their chosen area on the boat. When a glass was put down on the bar for a refill, it was lined up with the other glasses anxiously awaiting replenishment, and the rum bottle was turned upside down and passed over the glasses with a minimum of care. The bar and floor were awash with the spillage. Then a splash of everyone's favourite mix was added and the passengers wobbled away.

The conversation got louder and louder, the laughter became more pronounced, and not many people really cared about the beautiful lights of Aruba blazing on the island. As we toured the harbour and sailed past the resting cruise ships with their lights ablaze, I am certain that there were some people leaning over the sides of the ships watching and silently kicking themselves for not joining the party boat. To quote Disney, "Yo Ho, Yo Ho, a pirate's life for me!" It was fun, and a head count in the morning, even though some might have been twice the size that they would normally be, confirmed that the same number of people that got on the catamaran earlier in the day did in fact return.

Oh, yes, and the sunset was very nice.

Then it was on to Costa Rica where we were warned not to stray too far from the markets on the dock or from whatever excursion we had chosen. Evelyn and I decided to experience the rainforest. The six others decided they wanted to tour Costa

Rica to see the flora and fauna and a banana plantation. Once again, we got to see Ed in action before we left on our tour as the six of them decided they wanted to be adventurous and that the best way to see everything was to rent a small passenger van and driver. The price was clearly not going to be the first price quoted as the negotiation started. After considerable haggling, the six of them boarded the bus, along with the harried driver who seemed to be trying to decide whether or not he would be able to cover the cost of his gas. But he also seemed to be completely respectful of the tall, white-haired bargainer. Meanwhile, Ed was pretty pleased with himself for having arrived at a price that he considered to be *almost* fair.

Following the entertaining negotiation, Evelyn and I boarded a bus with a number of other people and started out on our journey. As we were travelling along on a bumpy road, presumably toward the forest, it occurred to me that they could take us anywhere. Similarly, the other six could end up somewhere they really didn't want to be. I guess it was the warning that had been implanted in my brain that set my imagination off on a tangent. We were just riding along on a bus with no clue what direction we are going or what our destination really was. I started to pay closer attention for any signs of forest or anything unusual and I was on edge for most of the journey.

As it turned out, we did end up in the forest, and the others let us know later that they had arrived safely at their destination as well. It was worth the small dose of anxiety. What an experience the rainforest was! Of course it's called a rainforest for a reason and we got a little wet, but the verdant foliage and the exotic birds we saw more than made up for it. We even saw poison dart frogs! I had visions of these little creatures standing on their hind legs and launching poisonous darts at us from incredible distances with even more incredible accuracy, like javelin throwers in the Olympics. Or maybe they would just spit them at us through tiny blowguns.

They actually get their name from tribes using the poison from the frogs to arm the tips of their arrows. The really dangerous ones are found in Colombia, so when our guides spotted them among the foliage, we were able to get a close look at their black and green colouring. Another sign that they are not totally vindictive is that they are coloured the way they are to warn other animals that they are poisonous. Awfully kind of them, really! I would love to spend more time in Costa Rica, but time and money are two of the enemies we battle in life for such amusements.

We sailed off again into the blue Caribbean Sea.

The next stop was the Panama Canal. For some reason, it doesn't seem to qualify as one of the seven manmade wonders of the world, but it's pretty amazing. The massive ship we were on scraped through with inches to spare on either side. Tractors called "donkeys" guided us through, and we passed a number of locks to get into the lake. At that point, we turned around back through the locks and were on our way home again.

As everyone seems to have exhausted their experiences on the Panama Canal cruise, Brenda is reminded of the trip she and Jim took to the Kingdom of Tonga. Tonga is somewhere between New Zealand and Hawaii in the South Pacific. It seems to be a land of friendly people! Brenda describes their journey:

"When we arrived at the airport in the Kingdom of Tonga, the temperature was 32 degrees and the humidity was over 90 percent. Our camera lens fogged over because of the change in temperature between the cool cabin air on the aircraft and the high humidity on the island. The high humidity was due to a cyclone that had just roared through the island two days previously. As we drove to the thatched-roof hut where we would be staying, we could see downed trees everywhere.

"We were looking forward to staying in a hut with a thatched roof as it is not something we're likely to do in Canada. The brochure advertised that all huts had central fans so we didn't expect heat to be a problem. Unfortunately, since the power grid had been taken out by the downed trees, the fans didn't work either.

"We rented an eleven-passenger van to tour the island. We were pretty noticeable as Tonga is not a tourist destination to begin with, and our visibility was heightened by the fact that we were the only Caucasians travelling around the island in a Fed Ex van. Because tourists are rare, there were very few places open to eat on a Sunday, but there were some incredible sights. They have flying fox bats, a cave system, and at least three miles of blowholes along the coast. The blow holes spurt water like Christmas lights coming on in a row, one after the other around the point and across the bay."

Ron, who had been intently reading his Western novel while listening to the story with mild interest, suddenly glances up over his glasses. "Did you say fox bats?"

"Yes, they're considered sacred in Tonga. With a wingspan of over three feet, they are the property of the king and no one can hunt them or harm them except royalty! I am not sure what the cyclone did to the bat population, though. There certainly seemed to be enough when we were there."

Most of those in the room shiver at the thought of giant bats. It's time for everyone to shift positions, look out the window, pour a cup of coffee, have another beer, and do whatever else people do every few hours. As we are wandering around, a brief discussion ensues about bats getting tangled in people's hair, especially women's. Since bat eyesight is considered to be better at night than it is in the daylight, we come to the conclusion that a bat would have no reason to entangle itself in someone's hair. Something to research on the Internet when we get home!

When everyone reconvenes, Brenda picks up the story about their Tonga visit. "When it was time to leave Tonga and as we were heading back to the airport, our van developed a flat tire about half way across the island. The spare was rusted into the carrier under the van and required brute force to break it loose. It didn't seem to have enough air pressure, and the jack was missing a piece of the handle so the crank had to be removed and reattached at every turn.

"A gentleman who was driving by stopped to welcome us to Tonga, noticed our predicament, and offered a young man who was travelling with him to help jack up the van. However, we couldn't find a rock to place in front of the wheel to prevent it from rolling forward. Ingenuity prevailed, and we used a rotting coconut from the roadside."

"See, I told you coconuts were misunderstood," I interject.

Ed points out, "At least your problem was solved."

"Not really," says Jim. "We attempted to put the flat tire on the carrier under the van. It wouldn't stay there after we had wrenched it loose so the flat tire rode with us to the airport in the wheel well beside the seats. The rusty catch wouldn't hold it there so we went into the bush beside the road, broke off some barbed wire, and twisted it around the catch to hold it closed. We then continued on our way, limping to the airport at forty kilometres an hour, arriving just in time to catch our flight."

Everyone seems to be silently considering the axiom about it being the destination, not the journey. I think we all convince ourselves that the van trip should be lumped in with the journey and that the destination was worth it. Brenda and Jim certainly think so.

23

AS IT ALWAYS DOES when men get together, talk eventually turns to golf. Or at least, I turned the conversation to golf because that's one of my favourite subjects. None of the others play, but the earlier story about Ron's exploits following the bouncing ball while playing mini-putt on the ship brought back some memories. As my travelling companions know, my friends and I are pretty avid golfers and we have taken a few road trips to Myrtle Beach for a week of golf. I remind the group about some of the experiences we have had there. One of my buddies walked into a concrete post and split his head open for a few stitches. Another rolled out of the cart on a turn, did a summersault worthy of at least a 9.8, and broke his wrist. Like a true Canadian, he continued to play for the week. He said, "What am I going to do? Sit in the hotel room?" I swear all of this happened *before* we had any beer.

This is an opportunity to share some more of my golf adventures, and maybe to cleanse my conscience a little. Unfortunately for a certain Canada goose recently, life will never be the same because of an errant shot on the golf course. Everyone knows about our famed Canadian export, the Canada goose. Canada's economy is driven by international trade and one of its greatest exports, although it doesn't attract many dividends, is the Canada goose. They're big and majestic with black heads and white chinstraps. Their long neck leads to a mostly brown body with white markings. They fly in V-formation and can be heard honking happily as they head for warmer climes. It's very similar to the Canadian people who head for the south, who are known as snowbirds. There is some connection there for sure. But there is one big distinction. The Canada goose leaves its droppings everywhere in vast quantities. Fortunately, snowbirds are a little more civilized.

The Canada goose could well be one of the least popular exports that Canada has. They are all over the golf courses where we play and they were in abundance recently when my friends and I played a round.

"There were probably thirty Canada geese between us and the hole on a short par three, lying around, honking, and eating. As I lined up my shot, they were not even in my thoughts. There are so many of them, they become like water or trees on a golf course. You just try to ignore them." My typical golf shot is not very long, but the height gives astronauts pause and could endanger the space station. It was not to be on this day. "I hit a screamer about twelve inches off the ground. Thud! Into the side of a Canada goose. It kind of flopped over, shook itself, and got up."

In spite of the fact they're not well respected and far from being endangered, I felt badly that I had hit it. I felt even worse when we walked up and noted its wing hanging to the side. I said to my golfing companions, "Do you realize that poor goose will not be able to fly south for the winter?" One of my more unsympathetic buddies said, "Do you realize some of our friends to the south would probably pay you for what you just did?" I apologized to the goose on the way by. When I got home, my wife suggested I should have mentioned it to someone, and one of her friends said that I should have killed it to put it out of its misery. Okay, now that's all I need! Can you imagine the course official driving up and seeing me bludgeoning a Canada goose with my 9-iron?

I'm not sure my story garners much sympathy for me or the goose. We're both left to nurse our respective injuries—mine emotional, the goose's physical. Evelyn empties the coffee maker for the third time and returns to the chair she claimed when this meeting started a few hours before. She and Linda have been making regular trips to the coffee pot and alternate making new batches. There's no danger of the coffee being less than fresh with those two around.

Evelyn had a milestone birthday in 2009 that she decided to celebrate with a friend on a cruise ship in the Caribbean Sea, visiting St. Thomas, San Juan, Antigua, and St. Martin. Our son Chris and I had decided that year that we would go to Africa to try to fight through fatigue, extreme exhaustion, and altitude sickness to climb Africa's tallest peak, Mount Kilimanjaro. It was a celebration of my sixtieth birthday, and the trip is fully documented with input from our son in our book, *Kilimanjaro and Beyond: A Life-Changing Journey*. Many people have questioned my sanity to be doing what I did while Evelyn was doing what she did. She settles in with her coffee and starts the story.

"My friend Beth, whom I hadn't spent any time with for about forty years, realized we wanted to go somewhere, and I convinced her to try a cruise. As this was to be her first cruise, Beth was a little apprehensive about the trip. Her husband was even more concerned so he wouldn't let us have a balcony as 'everyone who falls off a cruise ship apparently goes off that part of the ship.'"

"We had to meet the cruise ship in New York and we all piled into a tour bus to get there. I have a certain aversion to anything by Frank Sinatra. In fact, I told my son if he played anything by Frank Sinatra, he could play it anywhere but in the house. Well, since we were on our way to New York, what song do you think they played?" Everyone chimes in, "New York, New York." Evelyn nods and takes a sip of coffee, obviously trying to erase the memory of having to listen to that song and everyone singing along for hours on end.

The two women thought they would have nothing to talk about on their adventure since they hadn't spent any time together for a long time, but such was not the case. They also became intrepid adventurers as they struck out for Times Square after dark. "We wanted to see it with the lights on," Evelyn says. "There were people on the tour who were following us, thinking we knew where we were going. We had no clue. Once we found Times Square, the people following us started talking to us. They were surprised when we told them we had never been to New York before and had no clue where we were going. We were all happy we had found Times Square, had lunch together, and went our separate ways to continue our respective adventures."

As Evelyn continues her story, she recounts the experience of the cruise ship. "It was a geriatric cruise. There were more wheelchairs and scooters than you could count. If there was a scooter on the elevator, there was no way people were getting on. If there were people on the elevator, the scooters had to wait."

Evelyn mentions that Beth had her own special experience on the ship. "As we weren't allowed to go to our rooms immediately, we went for lunch first. After lunch when we arrived at our room, only my suitcase was there. Beth's was nowhere to be seen. We went for dinner, thinking it would show up but when we arrived back, there was still no suitcase. We decided to wait until morning before trying to track it down in the hopes that it would magically appear during the night.

"The next morning, I was awakened by the sound of the phone ringing. It was someone from another stateroom saying that there was a suitcase with Beth's name on it outside their door. Beth went to find it." As anyone knows who has been on a cruise ship it is often impossible to get there from here. "Even though the room with the missing suitcase sitting all alone outside its door was on the same floor as we were on, there was a skating rink in between, making it impossible for Beth to easily get there. After wandering around for a while, she finally found the front desk and asked for directions. The purser gave her directions and sent her on her way. She promptly got lost again."

We could just imagine Beth wandering around on the ship looking for any room with a suitcase outside its door and we were getting more and more amused, as people often do at the misfortunes of others. Evelyn takes another sip of coffee. "Beth returned to the front desk, and there were two ship employees there this time. When Beth explained her saga, one of them told her that she shouldn't have to find her suitcase by herself. She was relieved when the employee accompanied her to find the suitcase. They arrived at the end of the hall, and the employee asked Beth if that was her suitcase at the far end. Beth said it was. 'Good,' said the employee as he turned and went back to his post, leaving Beth to struggle with the suitcase."

Of course the story didn't end there. "She had to get it back to our room so, knowing that there was a skating rink between her and our room, she went up one floor. This time, it was the casino that was between her and our room at the other end of the ship. She trundled through the casino, dragging the suitcase behind her with more than a few eyes following her every step."

The personnel at the desk changed over quite frequently, and there seemed to be little communication among them. When Evelyn and Beth eventually returned to their room, there were seven messages waiting for them from different people asking if Beth had found her suitcase. The next time they returned, there were five or six more. Beth finally went to the desk (twice) to advise them that she did indeed find her suitcase.

The grins become wider as we all silently thanked our lucky stars that this hadn't happened to us. And as it turned out, there was some benefit to Beth spending so much time at the purser's desk. "When we were having breakfast several days later, I sat with two couples at one end of the table and Beth sat at the other with an elderly lady who was sitting by herself. To open the conversation, Beth asked the lady how her cruise was going. The lady said that it wasn't going very well because her husband had just died. Beth sympathized and asked how recently this had happened. The lady responded, 'Last night.'"

"The poor woman had been told to go for breakfast and that she would have to depart the ship at the next port of call to fly back to her home in Philadelphia. The husband would continue the cruise until the end. Since the woman was in shock and unable to function properly, Beth talked to her new friends at the purser's desk to make sure someone would be with the woman until she left the ship.

"In addition to the death, another older gentleman (weren't they all?) fell and broke his hip on the ship. The ship's crew didn't have a way of handling a broken hip onboard, so the poor man was confined to his stateroom, unable to move, for the duration of the cruise. As we arrived back at our home destination, there were police cars (so that the police could investigate the death and confirm that the deceased was a U.S. citizen), a coroner's van (to remove the body), and an ambulance (to take the man with the broken hip). We could not leave the ship until this triumvirate had been taken care of!"

There was one more bizarre situation that happened to these two adventurers. Evelyn picks up the story. "As usual on a ship, one night we were required to dress up for dinner so Beth and I put on our finest. We thought it would be fun to have our picture taken by someone else rather than paying a king's ransom to buy one of the photos taken at every opportunity by the ship's staff. We were waiting outside the dining room and decided that we would ask the first person to come along if they would mind taking our picture. A woman who was beautifully dressed was the first, and I approached her to ask if she would be our official photographer. I said, 'Would you mind taking our pic . . .' My voice trailed off. Then I said to her, 'Oh my, what lovely shoes!' The reason for my sudden change in conversation was that as I looked closer I noticed that the poor woman had no hands!"

Everyone in the room bursts out laughing. Of course, no one was laughing at the fact that the woman was unfortunate enough not to have any hands. We could only sympathize with that. What was funny was the situation. As Evelyn puts it, "What are the odds that of all the people on the ship we would ask the person least likely to be able to take a picture?"

Evelyn summarizes the trip. "In spite of the fact that we had to listen to Frank Sinatra on the bus there AND BACK, sail for two days before getting out of the cold weather, Beth getting lost on the ship, someone else being lost permanently, and we never did get our picture taken, it was an enjoyable trip. We guided a tour of unsuspecting people in New York, saw the walled city of San Juan, the Golden Lion Tamarin monkeys with their thick manes and the giant beaked toucan in the Commonwealth of Dominica, and went for a mini submarine ride in Barbados. And, we saw the ancient trees of Antigua."

But the most important thing is that good friends are able to pick up where they left off, no matter what the distance and time has been. Anyone lucky enough to have a handful of people like that in their lives is truly blessed, and Evelyn and Beth were like that. Evelyn reflects on her experience. "Although Beth and I thought we would have nothing to talk about, it was just the opposite. All in all, it was an amazing trip."

24

CAROL PULLS OUT her omnipresent journal and flips through the pages. As she does so, she says that one of her favourite trips was the bus tour of Italy combined with the cruise of the Mediterranean. "Do you want to know how much that trip cost?" Once again there is uncharacteristic unanimity among the group. "No!"

Carol's notes appear to be comprehensive. Although none of us feel compelled to do it, there would clearly be times when the notes would be valuable. It's not just a matter of keeping track of costs. It's a reminder of hotels that were good or bad (and believe me, that's important), whether the food at a particular restaurant is edible or not and at a price that is reasonable, and whether excursions taken are worth the price. For any traveller, this kind of information is invaluable. While there are websites that provide reviews, we aren't all the same. Opinions vary. It would be nice to be able to look back at notes to decide whether to go to the same place or do the same activity more than once. Having said that, Carol will probably continue to be the only one to do it.

There is the general feeling among everyone in the room that we want to travel so we use whatever spare cash we have to do that. It's a matter of priorities and, right now, this is the priority. Talking about how much a trip costs is of little interest to anyone at this stage. Well, except for Carol.

Carol continues to consult her notes. "Randy and Nadine joined us on this trip. It didn't get off to a great start as I recall. The airplane had mechanical difficulties in Toronto, and we were close to three hours late leaving. And then at the airport in Rome, the shuttle bus driver became embroiled in an altercation with the police about where he had parked the bus."

I GUESS WE MISSED THE BOAT

Ah, yes. We were all tired from the flight, but the adrenaline rush of being in Rome and the entertainment value of watching the police arguing with the bus driver in Italian kept us fully alert. Once we were under way, the first thing that became apparent was the traffic. It's bumper to bumper and side-by-side, stretching as far as the eye can see in both directions! The second thing was the scooters. They're everywhere. Weaving in and out of traffic, missing vehicles by inches and moving up to the front of the line waiting for the light to change, they seem to outnumber the cars. And if you are really adventurous, you can rent one! I don't think there is a single one of us who would consider doing that.

Since we were late arriving at the hotel, the group was half way through the introductions and the first excursion was being arranged—a walking tour by Trevi Fountain and the Piazza Navona. Evelyn and Brenda decided they didn't want to miss anything so, exhausted or not, off they went to toss some coins in the fountain and make a wish.

Rome is a magnificent city. And this bus tour was at a leisurely pace so we could sit back, enjoy the scenery, and take thousands of pictures. There was a thousand-year-old olive tree in front of our hotel! Before we left Rome, we toured the Sistine Chapel, the Coliseum, Circus Maximus, and St. Peter's Basilica. We were transported back in time, imagining the chariots, which probably inspired the chuckwagon races at popular rodeos around North America, careening around the track at Circus Maximus. The Coliseum was, of course, the scene of gladiatorial battles and public executions, among other things. It could hold fifty thousand people and is considered one of Rome's greatest architectural accomplishments. Gladiatorial battles probably led to North American football.

There was a great story told to us by the guide at the Sistine Chapel. The ceiling of the Sistine Chapel was, of course, painted by Michelangelo and it depicts the story of the bible in a series of frescoes. Apparently, it is over five thousand square feet, and there are over three hundred figures painted on the ceiling. It's possible to just stand there and stare all day at the ceiling, except for the inevitable crick in the neck. There are strict orders not to take photographs, and, of course, people who are either hard of hearing or just plain ignorant were snapping away.

According to the story, Michelangelo was happily painting away one day, which he did for some four years. I use the term "happily" loosely because the painter of the Sistine Chapel was actually a sculptor. However, the Pope of the day decided he wanted Michelangelo to paint the ceiling so he painted the ceiling. When someone doesn't really want to paint something (as we all know when our wives tell us that something in the house needs to be painted), four years to accomplish what he did is simply amazing!

So he was "happily" painting away when a Cardinal criticized his work. It just so happened that he was painting Judgment Day so he painted the critical Cardinal's face on the person depicted to be in charge of the underworld. It took twenty years for the Cardinal to notice, but when he did, he had a heart attack. He survived the heart attack and went to visit the Pope to ask that the face be changed. The Pope shrugged and said, "I'm sorry, but I'm only in charge of Heaven. I have no control over what happens in Hell."

There is a moral to this story, ladies. Never criticize a man in the middle of his painting!

As good as that story is I am a little skeptical about tales that have been passed down through the ages. I can remember lining up with some classmates to do an exercise in one of the early grades at school. The exercise was to determine how a story can change in a matter of seconds. The challenge was for the first person to whisper in the next person's ear, "The rain in Spain stays mainly in the plain." Each person was to repeat in a whisper in the ear of the person next to them what they had heard. The lineup was about eight kids long, and when the last person was asked to repeat what they had heard, it was something like, "The planes in Spain usually land in the rain." Of course, I am not exactly sure what the last person said because after this many years, I don't remember!

So, added to the fact that when we get into our so-called "golden years" we can't remember anything is the fact that a story can change in a matter of seconds as it passes from one person to another. So, how is it that we can believe that a three-thousand-year-old story is accurate!?? I guess they must have kept notes like Carol's back in those days as well!

Then we passed through the Italian countryside on our way to Venice. Past rows of pine trees (that actually provide pine nuts), olive trees, and grape vines, we made our way into the water town. There is always a wonderful feeling seeing something you have read about for years and there is a certain romanticism about Venice. Of course, we booked a gondolier ride because that is what everyone dreams about. There are just two people plus the gondola driver as you ride on the water under the sunshine with the gondolier gently pushing the pole into the water as the gondola glides along. The only sound you hear is the soft voice of the driver as he sings an Italian song in his soft voice. You're alone in Venice.

Actually, the sound we're hearing is another popular myth being debunked. There are, of course, hundreds of gondolas because they are Venice's biggest tourist attraction. We lined up along with other tourists from around the globe and were assigned a gondola along with Ed and Carol and Randy and Nadine. The actual sounds we heard were the gondola drivers bickering about space or talking on their cell phones. Once on the water, we were surrounded by other gondolas as we glided through the rippling waves. We did hear one gondolier singing, but he wasn't in our boat! But despite that, it's still wonderful to experience a gondola ride in Venice!

We didn't spend enough time in Tuscany but we did get a taste, so to speak, and made a mental note to go back. We toured San Gimignano, a walled medieval town with its cobbled streets in the province of Siena, Tuscany. The views from the highest tower in the centre of town overlooking Tuscany are simply unforgettable. The storekeepers in the town are unforgettable, too, as they are not particularly interested in showing you anything unless you are going to leave with a purchase.

In Florence, that guy Michelangelo popped into our tour again; his seventeen-foot-tall *David* is the talk of the town. Apparently, he's anatomically correct in every way, so other parts of his body are proportionate to his height. The ladies in the crowd were told to beware as once they had seen *David* they would never be interested by anything else. In fact, *David* is so special that there is an extra charge to go and see him. We didn't bother. There is a mini version of him in the square in Florence and also at an observation deck. There's a version of him in Buffalo, New York, and a number of other places. Jim points out that the guy gets around, but I guess when you're that, um . . . tall, you can do that!

Then it was time to board our cruise ship in Rome and head off on our Mediterranean cruise. The first stop was Naples, home of Pompeii and Mount Vesuvius. The weather was partially cloudy as I strained to catch a view of Mount Vesuvius. I have a fascination for mountains, and I chose a climb of Vesuvius combined with a tour of Pompeii for my excursion. Others chose a longer tour of Pompeii or a drive on the Amalfi coastline.

The climb up Vesuvius was led by a volcano expert who explained that it will erupt again but there are sensors all over the mountain that should give the residents below a little more warning than the poor people of Pompeii had. It used to be a twelve-thousand-foot mountain. After the blast it became two four-thousand-foot mountains. We weren't allowed to go right to the top but we were able to look into the crater at the vapours wafting up from below and, of course, to enjoy the inevitable souvenir shop at the end of our hike.

Pompeii is another world entirely. It was buried under thirteen to twenty feet of ash when Vesuvius erupted in 70 AD. Vesuvius is about five miles away. Residents of Pompeii who survived, if there were any, would have farther to go to the beach after the eruption as the ash filled in the sea for a considerable distance. In fact, we were told that excavation will begin along the outside walls of Pompeii where they expect to find and make casts of intact ships! One can only imagine what it must have been like for the people who lived there, and there are reminders. From the paved roads to the intricate plumbing systems and outdoor theatres, we are left to wonder again if we have really progressed that far.

I GUESS WE MISSED THE BOAT

Because the tour was a limited one, we had a choice between seeing the brothel and seeing the casts of some of the people and animals that died in the eruption. Our group chose the casts, although we did see the penis engraved in the concrete walkway pointing in the direction of the brothel. They had a flair for signage back then! We were told that the walls of the brothel are lined with frescoes of various sexual acts. The frescoes could have served as some kind of manual for the uninitiated, or simply put there for the enjoyment of the paying customers, or they could have been there to give the bored ladies of the evening something to look at over the shoulder of their companion.

The casts are absolutely eerie. People died where they sat. Perhaps the most disturbing is an obviously pregnant woman who is lying on her stomach, presumably to protect her unborn child and a dog that had apparently been chained at the time of the disaster. It obviously died in great pain. It's haunting to see. It's like the proverbial train wreck; it's almost impossible to avert your eyes, but there was an incredible quiet as we made our way through the exhibit and everyone was lost in their own thoughts.

At dinner back at the ship, everyone was talking about how pleased they were that they had chosen the excursion they did. The Amalfi Coast was stunning! You should have seen it! The long tour of Pompeii was amazing!! You should have gone on that excursion. I don't know which was best since I didn't experience them all. All I know is that I could spend much more time at Pompeii than I did and that climbing Vesuvius and learning about the disaster from an expert while standing on the scene of the crime was an experience I will never forget.

From there we moved on to the great city of Athens, Greece, where the churches, sculptures, architectural wonders, cars, scooters, and declining economy are concentrated. I think the fine art of picking pockets probably was honed long before the declining economy. With about eight thousand of our closest friends, we were on our way up to the Acropolis and the Parthenon when Ed was a near victim. He had his wallet tucked in a pocket of his shorts with a zipper and Velcro cover over it. The zipper was done up and the Velcro cover was closed.

We stopped at a crowded lookout along with the hordes of people that were moving along like zombies, and Ed felt something against his pocket. He brushed his hand against the pocket, and a few seconds later someone behind him handed him his wallet and said, "Here, I think you dropped this." He is quite certain that as he brushed his pocket, he knocked the wallet out of the would-be thief's hand. It could have been disastrous for Ed, and after that we all kept one hand on our wallet as we toured Athens.

The only thing more plentiful than the pickpockets are the scooters and they are everywhere, dodging anything that moves and some things that don't. Looking from the bus we'd see a helmeted head go by about half way between the window and the ground. The head is attached to a body that is usually dressed in a suit and tie. That body is firmly planted on a two-wheeled scooter. There is often a briefcase dangling along the side somewhere. It takes a certain amount of testicular fortitude to ride a scooter in Athens or Rome, and there seems to be a lot of that going around. As they wobble slowly by the bus, they practically scrape the sides. The entire purpose of this exercise is to make it to the front of the line so that they can charge ahead in unison as soon as the "go" sign is given. Then they are all off and running again on a life-threatening mission to get wherever it is they are going as inexpensively as possible.

Back on the cruise ship, we sailed to the Greek island of Mykonos. As we pulled into the port, we could see stacks upon stacks of white houses. We were able to do a little shopping. I enjoyed a Greek beer, and Evelyn ordered a baklava, which is very Greek, very rich, and very sweet. Being a bit of a health snob, I said I didn't want any . . . until I tasted it. Then the fight was on to see which one of us would get the bigger portion. We bought some souvenirs at a quaint little store and as we were leaving, I said, "Tikanis." Evelyn said, "I think that means 'how are you.'" Oh, well, it's all Greek to me.

Rhodes was the next island. It's known for its deadly vipers, although fires in the recent past have wiped out a good part of the population. It's an area also known for its beaches and tourists. We did see some beaches, but I can't really say we saw any vipers (thankfully) or a lot of tourists (but that's okay!). We visited the walled part of the city and then the ancient ruins of Kamiros, which once again had a maze of terracotta pipes carrying water for the population of the time. Cisterns held the water.

From there we sailed on the Mediterranean to the port of Kusadasi, Turkey. The tour took us to the Blessed Virgin Mary's house, which is probably one of the most serene places on the planet. There is a wall where people place their wishes and it's laden with ribbons. Setting aside the appearance of the apparition of the Madonna in the early 1900s and the reports of people being cured after drinking the holy water from the stream, it's a tiny house among the trees and it's just incredibly peaceful.

You do have to ignore the guards with their machine guns watching over the place. I thought about taking a picture of one guard but I didn't want the last photo I took to be of a bullet streaking toward me so I asked if I could. He grunted his agreement, but his eyes continued to scan the surroundings as I did. I suppose the bad guys would get some kind of satisfaction out of the symbolism of attacking the home and its surroundings. I can only assume that some sort of specific threat had been received, judging by the armed attention it was getting.

Then it was on to the ancient city of Ephesus. It's mostly ruins there now, although some of them are in great shape. Once again the "modern" conveniences are on display, such as terracotta plumbing and bathhouses. In fact, the latrine has constantly running water, and the wealthy took their toilet habits so seriously that they sent a slave to warm up the marble seat before they went to do their business. There were no privacy separations, and it was considered a social activity . . . if you can imagine. At least we can say that we have advanced to drinking coffee as our way of sharing the latest gossip.

The façade of the library is an architect's dream. With its columns upon columns and intricate design work, it looms up into the sky. It must have been a magnificent structure in its day. The amphitheatre, which held twenty-four thousand people for events that we can only imagine now, holds concerts for modern-day performers such as Pavarotti and Elton John. The acoustics are probably better than you would hear in a modern-day concert hall.

One sculpture that catches the eye is a triangular shape with one end supported by a large piece of stone. There is a beautiful woman carved on the surface of the triangular piece. She has wings and she appears to be flying with her robes flowing about her. Her arms and legs are muscular and she is holding a garland in her outstretched left hand. She is Nike, the winged Goddess of Victory, and the triangular shape of the relief carving brings to mind the Nike Swoosh symbol.

After sailing to the port of Alexandria, Egypt, we found ourselves bouncing along an Egyptian highway to Cairo. It seems that traffic is a constant object of discussion while travelling, and Egypt is certainly no exception. My fellow travellers and I have discussed the horns in Jamaica and the scooters in Greece and Italy. The traffic in downtown Dar es Salaam, Tanzania, Africa, is covered in Chris's and my book, *Kilimanjaro and Beyond*. It isn't so much the quantity of traffic in Egypt. Oh, sure, the cars are plentiful, old, and dilapidated. But what set apart the traffic in Egypt are the rules of the road. There don't appear to be any! When we were returning from Cairo after visiting the pyramids, the police had a car pulled over at the side of the road. What could the driver have possibly done? Since there are no rules of the road, or if there are, no one follows them, how could this person have broken the rules? Maybe it was a shakedown to provide the police officer with a little extra cash or the driver committed the token traffic misdemeanor of the day. I remain befuddled.

Ah, the pyramids! We have arrived. This is the wow factor. You study them in school. You see them in books and on television off and on your whole life. You wonder how they got there. And there they were, rising in their sun-drenched golden glory. Some are weather beaten, some have had pieces knocked off and stolen. But we were still standing at Giza just outside of Cairo on the desert sand observing one of the manmade wonders of the world.

There may not be rules of the road but there are unspoken rules at Giza. If you want to take a picture of a local on a camel, it will cost you. If you want a picture with a heavily armed security guard, you can do that . . . for a price. If you want to go for a camel ride, you can pay and they will take you. But they may take you out into the desert and threaten to leave you there if you don't pay to come back. I was urged to go out on a parapet of one structure to get a better view of the desert, which I did at no cost. But I noticed people trying to get back had to pay. I waited until a couple fumbled around in their pockets for some change and skipped around the person with his hand out. The tourists play a game by jockeying to take pictures of the pyramids at exactly the moment when a camel and its rider happen to be passing in front, just to avoid having to pay.

We ventured down into the depths of one tomb-like structure, and it was stifling hot. In fact, it was so hot that people were feeling faint. You could wait it out and leave through the exit, hoping you didn't pass out or become so sick that you would be added to the collection of people entombed there, or you could go back out through the entrance, at a cost of course.

The entrepreneurial spirit is alive and well in Giza.

Not far from the pyramids of Giza sits the magnificent Sphinx in quiet repose. I couldn't wait to get there. It's gigantic but a little weird looking. It has the body of a lion, the head of a cat, and the face of a person. Or something like that. Its nose has been shot or pried off giving it a distorted look and apparently it once had a beard, which has long since disappeared. Erosion has contributed some deterioration to give it even more character. It sits on its haunches like a satisfied cat with enormously long front paws, measuring about a third of its entire length. I am sure if it came to life for a few minutes, its tail would be drifting back and forth in contentment, completely satisfied with itself for having safeguarded the pyramids all these years. I am not sure it should be quite so smug, given that pieces of the pyramids have been stolen or vandalized right under its nose. But who am I to judge?

The most popular photo of the Sphinx is when it's lined up with the largest of the pyramids so you can see the triangular structure over the cat/human's right shoulder. Despite its flaws, it's an incredible sight.

On the way back from Giza, our guide let us know that there are children learning to make carpets and working in carpet factories. That will be their lifelong job. They start early in life and that's what they're destined to do. Our immediate Western reaction is to become indignant and shout, "Child labour practices." But these are children of very poor parents. The reality is they would not be going to school because their parents can't afford to send them. They would become street urchins, begging for food or possibly prostituting themselves to survive for a shortened life span. They would be lost in the dregs of humanity. By having a job, they may never be the chalk writing on the blackboard of life but they won't just be the dust either. It may not be ideal to be expected to make carpets but even at the age of twelve, it gives them some hope for the future and, most important, a sense of self-worth as they are doing something useful and meaningful. We all need to try to put ourselves in others' shoes before freely making pronouncements on situations we can't completely understand.

Then it was back on the cruise ship to the Greek island of Corfu where we sampled their wine and that well-known symbol of Greek culture, Ouzo. We toured some caves by boat, and with the sun shining through various openings in the rocks, the water was the bluest blue you can ever conjure up. It was a happy blue! It also highlighted our way forward, beckoning us into a labyrinth of stalagmites and stalactites. The Greek islands that we saw are wonderful exemplars of beauty and tranquility and they silently invite you back for more exploration, fulfillment, and relaxation.

As our ship makes its way back to Rome, there is one more anomaly that seems rather striking. There is a narrow passageway that goes between Italy's boot and Sicily. Once our ship squeezed through the narrow strait, we passed a cone-shaped island with its peak rising above the sea. Houses could be seen dotted among the vegetation at the base of the island, and it boasts a population of up to 850 people. The only way on or off is by boat with the nearest land a few miles away. Sounds idyllic, right? It's peaceful and private with no one to bother the inhabitants.

But it's what the residents on the island of Stromboli see when they look up that's startling. Running down from the mouth of the peak are visible lava flows with their dark colours in contrast to the blue shade of the island. It's an active volcano and it emits a relatively constant stream of vapour. Apparently, it's almost always active, although the most recent *major* eruption was in 2009. There are people living about three thousand vertical feet from impending disaster! I suppose it's some kind of risk/reward thing, but I don't get it.

We are nearing the end of our "meeting"—it will soon be time for us to go to the airport and then home to our different parts of the country. As we prepare to depart, I talk about the pinnacle of my travel adventures—my two trips to the part of the world previously known as the Dark Continent: Africa.

25

WHILE WE HAVE all talked about places to which we would like to return, there are obviously more places to see than there is time and money. But one place I will definitely revisit is Tanzania, Africa. After my climb of Africa's highest mountain, Mount Kilimanjaro, in 2009 with our son Chris, and our visit to meet the children for whom we were raising money, I found that I didn't choose Tanzania; Tanzania chose me. Linda nods her head. "Yes, you talk about that in *Kilimanjaro and Beyond*. What did you mean exactly?"

I was so taken by the children and their plight and how happy they were, even with the difficult circumstances they find themselves in, and I realized we could really make a difference with a little bit of effort. The country is dusty and impoverished, but the people are friendly and giving of themselves. In some cases, they have nothing. Some have unbelievably difficult family situations where the head of the house is a fourteen-year-old because the parents have died of HIV/AIDS. Yet, they persevere without complaint. When Evelyn and I went back in 2011 to see the finished well and classroom for which we had raised money, we met some young women who are absolutely delighted to be able to earn a living and provide for their families. The whole adventure has been a journey that truly has been life changing, and I want to continue to help where I can.

There were highlights of the trip that are recounted in our book. But perhaps one of the more humorous moments occurred in 2011 when we met the children at their school. Our Youth Group at the local church had prepared letters in English for the kids in Tanzania. Each had a red maple leaf drawn on the front, one of the symbols of Canada. Many of the letters referred to Canada's national pastime — hockey, and the National Hockey

I GUESS WE MISSED THE BOAT

League. You know that league where the rich players were on strike because the even richer owners had locked them out? Anyway, it came time for me to present the letters from our Canadian youth to the kids in Tanzania. I was speaking in English, and our translator was translating into Swahili for the kids.

Things were going swimmingly. I was doing my job by talking to them, and Tanga, our translator, was doing his job by translating. Then I mentioned the maple leaf and waited. Nothing! Tanga was standing a bit behind me and to my right. I turned to look over my shoulder to see what had happened to the translation. Had Tanga left the building? He looked at me a little perplexed and shrugged. He whispered, "I don't know what a maple leaf is." I thought about it for a second and just replied, "It's a big leaf from a Canadian tree." He smiled and got a laugh from the kids when he translated it into something they could understand.

We were off and running again. A little more about Canada; a little more translation. Then I mentioned hockey. Silence again. I stumbled around for a minute. I talked about ice in a drink but didn't seem to be getting far with that either. Finally, I said it's like soccer only it's played with sticks. Tanga simply wrapped his arms around his body and said, "B-r-r-r!" That brought a few nods and grins, but I'm still not sure they knew what the heck this stark white guy from Canada was talking about!

We were fortunate enough to go on a safari at the end of our last trip to Tanzania. Our guide spoke little English but he knew where to find the animals and he had books with descriptions of every species you could imagine. We were in a truck with an open top so that we could stand and see 360 degrees. Within five minutes of entering the Serengeti, we were greeted by giraffes and zebras. It is a wonderful sight to see them in their natural habitat. Why they hang around the road when they have thousands of square miles to roam is beyond me, but we were fortunate to see them.

One of our sons asked when we got back which of the animals was the coolest. The ultimate in cool is the big cat, of course. We were told that we may not see any because they were being particularly shy but we saw two males sleeping in a ditch and another lying in the shade of a tree. In both cases, the female was lying nearby waiting patiently to catch a meal. Uh, oh! There is a theme developing here. The males are asleep and the females are catching dinner. Minefield alert! I think that subject is best left unexplored.

A family of warthogs wandered by the female, but she was more interested in a gazelle that was a little farther away and probably a bit tastier. Certainly, it was better looking. Can you imagine waking up after being born and discovering you're a *warthog*? The disappointment would only get worse as you take in the animals surrounding you. "Mommy, am I good looking?" "Uh, yes, dear." Oh, well, I am sure they have nice personalities.

While the big cats are cool, for sheer awesomeness you can't beat animals that are bigger than the truck we were riding in. The elephants are plentiful and huge. The hippos are usually submerged in the water, but we did manage to catch sight of a mother and her baby out of the water. The baby was only the size of a half-ton truck. The rhinos are difficult to spot, but we took a couple of pictures of two that were barely visible even though my lens was fully extended.

For a few brief moments, I coveted the three-foot-long lenses that some people were lugging around, although I didn't envy the sore muscles they would surely have at the end of the day. When a female lion plopped herself down in the shade of one of the safari trucks after we interrupted her hunt, we enjoyed getting pictures that had to be of equal calibre to the ones taken by the lenses that almost touched her as the photographers leaned over the edge of the truck.

There's beauty everywhere in Tanzania, and part of that beauty is the animals that claim an equal share of the country. Upon waking up in the Serengeti, we could hear the baboons on the roof of the hotel. The staff did warn us at the front desk to keep our windows closed! The creatures can be vicious; their honesty is questionable as they will grab anything that is worth grabbing, but they are still fun to watch as they scramble on the rooftops and rocket through the branches.

I GUESS WE MISSED THE BOAT

But it was looking out on the plains from a hillside early in the morning that was truly awe inspiring. There was a sea of acacia trees standing guard over the plains and a light mist was hovering around the base of the trees, making for an eerie morning atmosphere. The tendrils of the mist wafted in and out of the acacias. The sun was just starting to heat up the day and casting shadows across the plains. Eventually, the sun would warm up the area sufficiently that the mist that sustains life for the vegetation would burn off for another day. While the tops of the trees meet and create a canopy protecting the floor below, there is movement above the tree line to the left. A giant head, which is attached to a beautifully patterned neck, can be seen bobbing above the tree tops. First one, then several more giraffes can be seen calmly munching away on the leaves that are their domain as nothing else can reach to that height.

The first animal we saw as we passed through the gates of the Serengeti was the incredible giraffe. They happily dine on the acacia trees that are adorned with thorns longer than the needles that my two sisters-in-law with their medical backgrounds have been known to plunge into people. The faces of the giraffes are pretty and they seem to thrive on that knowledge. I'm sure they take minimal time to put on their makeup in the morning, but their soft facial features, magnified by their dark doe eyes, long natural lashes, and full lips forming a permanent self-satisfied smile, might be the envy of any model strutting down the runway. Research has determined that men are attracted to full lips more than any other feature, so giraffes have to be on their guard constantly, especially from basketball players. But as they come close to the truck to afford the tourists a good look, they seem to be saying, "Look at me! I'm sexy and I know it."

Of course, God gave us all challenges, and the beautiful people (or animals) of the world face their own issues. The beautiful giraffe can't go down into Ngorongoro Crater to play with the other animals because as it is descending into the crater on its long, ungainly legs, it would topple forward and roll down the hillside in a tumbling mass of long legs, even longer neck, and a ball of patterned fur, landing spread eagle on the crater floor in an embarrassing heap. If it survived the fall, it would never be able to get out again as its long front legs would push its head back over its backside so it would constantly be toppling backwards. It would just be in a constant state of frustration and nobody deserves that, and I mean no-body! So, the beautiful giraffe has to find its thorny acacia elsewhere and satisfy itself with its stunning good looks.

A family of elephants in Lake Manyara National Park also amazed us. There, by the side of the road, stood Mom, Dad, and baby and, though they looked us over for a few minutes, their primary objective was to devour most of the living vegetation in the area. We could only see the bull elephant's ears flapping as it stood mostly hidden from view. It didn't seem to be too concerned when its camouflage slowly disappeared as it demolished each branch, one giant mouthful at a time. When you're that big, why should you be?

As we were driving toward Lake Manyara National Park and nearing the end of our safari, we couldn't get the passenger door shut. This would not do, so our fearless driver got out, and tried to fix it . . . with virtually nothing in the way of tools. He did manage to get the panel of the door off, and it looked like it had been fixed once or twice before. I am not sure exactly what the repairs were made with, but it was something akin to baler twine and chicken wire.

While he was working away, we were pretty much in the middle of nowhere. A van full of locals did drive by with its occupants hanging out every window and door. It was jammed to the roof, which in turn was loaded with a variety of packages. The van looked like a reject from the seventies, painted in every conceivable colour, and it roared along the road belching a stream of bluish-black smog. Of course, had it been *in* the seventies, the sounds of Jefferson Airplane would have been blasting and the smoke would have been coming from the *inside* of the van. The Africans used every usable space of that van, and then some.

It was a little disconcerting being stuck there while our driver did the best he could with what he had. The anxiety amped up a little more when two mean-looking women carrying huge machetes walked by. We tried to avoid eye contact, although from the corner of my eye I could see them glaring and swinging the machetes. Fortunately, they kept walking, and miraculously, with a little ingenuity, luck, and possibly chewing gum, the door was fixed and we were on our way to see more of nature's beautiful creatures.

It's hard to believe that we got to the point where our reaction was that it was just another elephant but that's what happened. Still, there is nothing like seeing animals in their natural habitat. With the vehicle parked in the Serengeti, we could look across the expanse of the endless plains and see nature unfold before our eyes. There were herds of animals, some grazing, some sleeping, and some just walking, apparently aimlessly, although undoubtedly with some purpose in mind. Of course, I use the term "herd" lightly as it could have been a tower of giraffes, a bloat of hippopotamuses, a memory of elephants, or any of the other colourful descriptions that someone has dreamt up in their infinite wisdom. The ones that were born to be hunters were hunting, and the prey was forever on its guard, trying to stay alive for another day. The sleepers sleep in circles, but there are always sentries staying awake to alert them if danger lurks. It's beautiful and awe inspiring to watch and it's frightening to think that's how they live out their lives. It's also depressing to think that there are many humans throughout the world, who are supposed to be more intelligent, living out their lives the same way.

But eventually, we tourists get tired; I was suffering from the consequences of having messed up my cholera medication before leaving, and it was time to go. While I didn't have cholera, I probably wasn't properly protected and I did catch some form of illness that left me dragging my Canadian butt around Africa on the final stages of our trip.

Our flight home was another one of those endurance tests that only seasoned travellers can abide. It was forty-eight hours of travel from the time we started the journey until we walked in our front door. Note to self: Stop in Amsterdam overnight next time. You're not getting any younger, you know!

The group is getting a little restless, milling about in the room and checking the tags on their luggage in anticipation of leaving soon. The saying goes that all good things come to an end, and it's time to head north to the cold from the beautiful Florida sunshine after spending just a little more of the kids' inheritance.

As Evelyn pointed out at the beginning, the real benefit of travel is the learning experience. I'm not exaggerating when I say that travel has changed my life. Trevor said recently that I went up one side of a mountain as an accountant and I came down as a philanthropist. It's an apt description. While travel around the world has left an indelible impression on me, having seen the plight of the children of Africa firsthand and going back a second time to observe the difference some assistance can make, has changed me forever. With the help of a lot of people, Evelyn and I have raised over $100,000 since 2009 to help provide clean water and a classroom for a community in Mwanza, Tanzania. The latest project is to raise money to help young women and youth in Tanzania start small, sustainable businesses.

Everyone in this group in Miami has been places where the inhabitants struggle to survive on virtually nothing. We've learned that we all have a role to play in fixing that. The biggest need these desperate people have is opportunity. They should have the same opportunities that we were fortunate enough to be born with, like clean water and education. Giving them things is not the answer. For example, building big box stores in impoverished countries doesn't help, in my opinion, because they may employ a few people but they take the entrepreneurial spirit to start small businesses away from the majority. It's the opportunity to get started on a self-sustaining life full of promise and fulfillment that is needed the most.

We can learn so much from others about appreciating what we have. We live in one of the greatest countries in the world and we are reminded of that every time we travel. But we have to ensure we don't fall victim to a sense of entitlement that's

I GUESS WE MISSED THE BOAT

easy to do simply *because* we live in one of the greatest countries in the world. Evelyn reminds us of an example: "We had just returned to our middle-class neighbourhood from seeing people struggle with a lack of clean water. There was a water ban in our area because of a broken water main, and residents were complaining bitterly about being unable to wash their cars. It put things into perspective."

We can all do our bit, whether it's just taking small amounts of the basic necessities to a resort, or taking soccer balls to a school or sponsoring a child. But it has to be done with common sense. Wells must be drilled to provide clean water for sure but they must be sustainable by the locals. Classrooms must be built so the opportunity exists for children to become educated, but the capacity must also exist locally to maintain them. The opportunities must be available so that everyone can have meaningful lives and a sense of pride and accomplishment.

There is no greater eye opener than travel. It can be shocking and overwhelming but it can also be educational and enlightening. It's worth the effort to set aside a little extra throughout a career to have the opportunity to experience what we have. It's also valuable to just get away to relax and unwind. It replenishes us for whatever life has to send our way next. It can be truly life changing.

And apparently, it leaves us with stories to tell.

It's time to go and everyone grabs their belongings. Linda has time for one more smoke when she gets outside; Carol's notebook is resting at the top of her purse, easily accessible so she can record the cost of the shuttle to the airport. Evelyn is anxious to see the grandchildren but she forces a few more drops out of the coffee maker since Linda had already nearly emptied it. Brenda is laughing at something Jim just said, and Ed is preparing himself to negotiate the next financial transaction. Ron is looking forward to getting back to see the horses. As for me, I enjoy being in different places and travelling with this group. I also enjoy being surrounded by my "stuff" at home.

Jim gets the last word as we pick up our carry-ons and, dragging our luggage, head for the door to catch the flight back to our respective winter climates. We've learned that it doesn't do any good to hug the street lamps in the hopes that we won't have to go home yet. We'll still have to suffer through days and weeks of winter but we know the light at the end of the tunnel isn't a train this time. There will actually be hope when we get home that spring is just around the corner. There will be warmer days, the snow will be starting to disappear, and there may even be the odd spring flower poking up through the ground in places.

We're not looking forward to one more airport and everything that entails. But sensing the complaining is about to start, Jim puts it all in perspective. "I'm not sure why people complain about flying. It used to take weeks and months to travel across the country. They had to ride in covered wagons in the freezing cold, bumping along on ground that had not been cleared to accommodate any kind of conveyance. People got sick and died. Babies were born. And they weren't escaping from their daily routine for a few days. That *was* their daily routine! Now we can go across country in a relatively comfortable seat, watch a movie or two, have a nap, and we're home."

It's time to go and we quietly head out the door.

Meeting adjourned!

About the Author

PHOTO BY ROBIN CHU

In 2009, Barry Finlay went up a mountain as an accountant and came down a philanthropist. After over thirty years in various financial roles with the Canadian federal government, he took his life in a different direction and climbed Africa's Mount Kilimanjaro at age sixty with his son Chris. The climb and their fundraising efforts to help kids in Tanzania led to the award-winning book, *Kilimanjaro and Beyond: A Life-Changing Journey*. Barry has since been named to the Authors Show's list of "50 Great Writers You Should Be Reading." In 2013, he received the Queen Elizabeth Diamond Jubilee medal for his philanthropic work in Africa.

For more information, visit
http://www.keeponclimbing.com/